The Making of Macau's Fusion Cuisine

The author would like to thank IEEM, the Institute of European Studies (Macau), for funding the research for this book.

The author would also like to acknowledge the Guild of Food Writers (London) for financial support in respect of the fieldwork carried out in Malacca in July 2018.

The Making of Macau's Fusion Cuisine

From Family Table to World Stage

Annabel Jackson

Hong Kong University Press
The University of Hong Kong
Pok Fu Lam Road
Hong Kong
https://hkupress.hku.hk

© 2020 Hong Kong University Press

ISBN 978-988-8528-34-9 (*Paperback*)

All rights reserved. No portion of this publication may be reproduced or transmitted in any form or by any means, electronic or mechanical, including photocopying, recording, or any information storage or retrieval system, without prior permission in writing from the publisher.

British Library Cataloguing-in-Publication Data
A catalogue record for this book is available from the British Library.

Digitally printed

In fond memory of PK
(1949–2013)

Secret Family Recipes
by Professor Leung Ping-kwan
(written in Chinese and translated into English by Brian Holton)

the swirling flicker begins from a lamp
an always unsustainable accident at your ear
some say you're hot-tempered but you're already
no longer that; people from later on
boiled that dish dry, forgot
the original theme, as we stirred
we slowly lost ourselves
too vague, too weak, too compromised
impossible to arrive at the shape of the dawn-to-dusk thought
from beyond a mediocre cuisine we keep on wanting
to recover those lost notes

no matter where we go we always carry with us
from our youth the aromas that drifted through
lanes and alleys from big colonial houses after school
from the faraway town, renewing our desires
the comforting embrace we repeatedly lose
grown up, the subtly sweet and bitter sourness
disclosed in unavoidable depression
the secret escape route whose direction is unknown
eternal secret, stuck between the teeth like
Granny's paradoxical fishcakes
an undifferentiable blend of sweet and salty

if you have the best bacalhau, if you have
Portuguese olive oil, strong enough and mellow enough
can everything then be magically reproduced?

the dinners our godmothers cooked for us on Sundays
in every attic, behind every closed curtain and
shutter inside southern European-style windows
in these dusty yesterdays, what was so subtly shining?
sisters recorded it, kith and kin noted it down
and the paper slowly and gradually faded
impossible to hold on to these mysterious rites
performed with such wizardly perfection

remember the flavours of aniseed and nutmeg
those *balichão* stir-fries really mouth-watering
remember Granny used to cook a mysterious dish
(neighbours all knew in the kitchen she'd do her stuff)
the aroma was a lingering one, but after she had gone
there was no-one who could blend the same flavours again
our nickname was *muchi-muchi*, and after school
whoever lost a bet invited the other to eat *cha-cha* sweet bean soup
we grew up between meals, faintly remembering
grown-ups had shown us a mysterious album
we just mix food in the pan, not knowing if we can reclaim those riches

This poem was written for, and first published in *Taste of Macau: Portuguese Cuisine on the China Coast* (Hong Kong University Press, 2003).

Contents

Foreword	viii
Preface	ix
Acknowledgements	xi
Introduction	1
1. Macanese Food and Cultural Identity	15
2. Macanese Food in Macau	24
3. The Loss of a Cuisine and the Practice of Recipe Sharing	41
4. All at Sea: The Spread of Portuguese Culinary Influence across Asia	60
5. Towards a Definition of Macanese Cuisine	80
Conclusion	114
Appendix 1: Background and Methodology	126
Appendix 2: Diaspora and the Casa Movement	130
Notes	139
References	143

Foreword

I first met Annabel in Hanoi in 1996, when she was researching her Vietnamese cookbook *Street Café Vietnam*. This was an important book, particularly given that it was to be released just as the twenty-five-year American embargo was being lifted. This event was to put Vietnam back on the international map, after the country had been isolated for so many years. It was highly colourful book, with all essential recipes included, and Annabel captured many of the iconic dishes.

As an ethnic mutt (Egyptian Chinese), I have always been curious as to how others like me integrate. I am often asked why I haven't fused Egyptian and Chinese food. For me, they could only do so out of some kind of necessity. I wouldn't wish to mess with two great cuisines and turn them into a four-letter word—and I'm not spelling 'nice' here.

One only needs to visit Portugal to understand and appreciate the extent of the nation's colonial conquest. What they left behind seems so incorporated into other societies that it seems natural and normal, but the dishes are fusions of Africa, the spice trade, parts of India, and more.

This is the sort of book that I yearn for to gain a deep historical and cultural understanding of a place. It's a great reference work that will give you golden nuggets of information, which will leave you wiser and more informed than most.

As a half-Chinese person, it's very hard to imagine that the iconic egg custard tart isn't a Chinese creation but rather a Portuguese invention. It's just as shocking when you think that it was the Portuguese who taught the Japanese how to do tempura... that the Portuguese introduced the British to tea... and the chilli to Asia.

On these pages are discoveries that are fascinating to any food lover and will reveal the importance of Macanese cuisine. When I think of world cuisine and the fusion of countries that boast a great food culture, what generally comes to mind is Turkish incorporating Persian, Vietnamese, Malaysian/Singaporean, and Indian. But after reading this book, you will recognise the contribution of Portugal and Macau.

Bobby Chinn
April 2019
Restaurateur, chef, TV presenter, cookbook author, and world traveller

Preface

Amuse Bouche

In late autumn 2015, in the historic city of Perpignan in the foothills of the French Pyrenees, I attended a conference on European cuisines that was organised by the European enogastronomic brotherhood, which goes under the acronym CUECO. I had been invited to deliver a three-minute presentation on the 450-year history of Macanese cuisine, roughly defined as the Portuguese-based cuisine from a coastal region of the South China Sea. Given the unique status of the strongly Portuguese-based indigenous cuisine of Macau it represents, the Macanese Gastronomy Association in Macau is qualified to be a member of this European brotherhood.

After the speeches, and alongside categories such as 'artisan food producer of the year', 'food festival organiser of the year', and 'winery of the year', I was to receive the award for 'communicator of the year', based on my work on Macanese cuisine. This was something of a crowning glory—an accolade to mark the quarter century over which I have been writing about the unique cooking of the Macanese people as well as the broader sweep of Macau culinary culture.

A few weeks after this awards ceremony, I was invited by a small university in Macau, the Institute of European Studies (IEEM), where I had previously taught part-time on the subject of Macanese cuisine within a postgraduate diploma in cultural tourism, to apply for funding to pursue a further tranche of research and writing on Macanese cuisine as it related to bridge-building between East and West. I was fortunate enough to be awarded that funding—and this book is based on that research paper.

In my acceptance speech at the Perpignan conference, I thanked the Macanese community for granting me honorary Macanese status and for honouring me as a spokesperson for their culinary culture: I had given papers at a number of conferences in Hong Kong and Macau before presenting in France. I do feel that I have a special connection to Macau, and in that sense perhaps I am an honorary Macanese or at least a 'Macau person'. During the course of this research, expressions of a deep attachment to Macau, as told to me by several Macanese respondents, have very much mirrored my own attachment to the place and its historic culture.

Macau has—politically, culturally, economically, and, owing to land reclamation, even physically—changed dramatically, particularly within the last two decades. One almost wants to close one's eyes when driving along the Cotai Strip with one side part-Venetian, complete with gondolas, part-French, with a mini Tour Eiffel, and then the strangely themed (is that a giant plastic cactus?) Holiday Inn on the other. The once sleepy and once seemingly far-away Coloane Village with its little bank and its little post office has been encroached upon by apartment blocks and thereby almost (almost!) robbed of charm. The quietly grand downtown Largo de Senado, where once you might have stopped for a coffee and a tecelada (like a sweet omelette), is today too packed with tourists for locals to even think about a stroll there of an evening.

* * * * * *

My own first landing in Macau, 450 years after the Portuguese, was on my birthday in June 1989. Later, as the weekly restaurant reviewer on the *South China Morning Post* in the early 1990s (under the pen name of Wai Sik), I was introduced, via a friend in the art world, to a new restaurant in Macau. Whitewashed, it had interesting art on the walls and was strategically situated on the ground floor of the Hoi Fu Gardens residential block, a building particularly popular with Portuguese expats. This restaurant was called Balichão, and it was on meeting the owner that I became aware of a fascinating cuisine of global interest that had hitherto been more-or-less hidden away even within Macau itself: Macanese cuisine, the indigenous cooking of Macau. The restaurant owner was Isabel Eusebio, and it is to her that I am indebted for the avenues along which my fascination for the culinary culture of Macau have taken me, and in particular that of Macanese gastronomy. 'Annabel,' Isabel said to me on our first meeting, 'our cuisine is dying. Please help us.'

I went on to publish my first book on the food culture of Macau in 1994. It was entitled *Macau on a Plate* and focused on the then three main strands of eating culture in Macau: Cantonese, Portuguese, and Macanese. I believe this is the first time that Macanese cuisine was specifically singled out and written about in a book. In 2003, I wrote the first fully-fledged Macanese cookbook to enter the market: *Taste of Macau: Portuguese Cuisine on the China Coast*. I reworked this as an iBook, for Apple types, in 2013.

Now we embark on something altogether more academic.

Acknowledgements

First, I thank Dr José Luis Sales Marques, president of IEEM, the European Institute of European Studies in Macau, whom I have known for many years and who invited me to apply for funding to undertake a gastronomy research project that linked Europe and Asia—in other words, Macanese cooking.

Not unconnected, I also thank the Macanese Gastronomy Association in Macau, and in particular its president Luis Machado, for putting me forward for the CUECO award which helped to raise the profile of Macanese cuisine, and additionally led to this funding.

In London, thanks to Professor Michael Hitchcock, whom I first met in Macau, for not only supervising me on my initial research paper, but for his ongoing support. Thanks to Valerie Mars and Professor Gerald Mars for their interest in this project; and to Chef Vivek Singh and Chef Norman Musa for their insights.

I have been writing about Macanese cooking culture for about twenty-five years, and I want to thank all the Macanese in Macau, as well as the Macanese in the diaspora, who have warmly welcomed me, tirelessly cooperated with my research, and openly shared with me.

In Macau. I much regret that I have lost touch with her, for it was Isabel Eusebio who first got me interested in the Macanese and their cuisine. I adored the lawyer and novelist Henrique de Senna Fernandes, who left us in 2010 and with whom I shared so many great conversations (and cups of coffee); and his daughter Marina has given me so much of her time too. So have Sonia Palmer and Luis Lobo. Several Macanese have become personal friends, including Hugo Bandeira, Anabela Estorninho, Isabel da Silva, Vanessa Estorninho, and Carlos Marreiros.

Beyond Macau. Former lighting designer and now historian and prolific writer Tony da Silva, in California, never seems to tire of my questions. I cannot thank him enough, and I've been fortunate enough to share victuals with him in Hong Kong and Macau. In Hong Kong, many thanks to Patrick Rozario; and elsewhere in the Diaspora particular thanks to Graça Pacheco Jorge, Ed Rozario, and Nuno Prata Cruz.

Finally, thanks to all the Macanese who completed the SurveyMonkey questionnaire, most of whom I have never met and some of whom I have gone on to communicate with me privately. I hope I can meet many more of you in the future.

In Malaysia. How much I've appreciated your input: Jeffrey Hantover (well, via New York!), Tan Siok Choo, Walter Cheah, Lim Swee Kiang, Sara Frederica Santa Maria, Colin Goh, Tan Hing Sen, Chef Tan Poh Chuan at TPC Home Café in Malacca, Homestay hosts in Kampung Ayer Limau, Jenny Ahmad, and Zohaime bin Muhamad Sori; and my very, very special thanks to Chef Melba Nunis, and her family.

Thanks to Tourism Malaysia UK for conducting a half-day culinary tour of Kuala Lumpur; and to Tourism Malacca for help in meeting so many people, and in eating so many different kinds of food.

Introduction

> Food is a tangible entity that has stood through the test of time amidst the disappearing social norms, ceremonies, and rituals. (Ng and Sharim 2016, 104)

This book is partly based on the findings of a tranche of research undertaken between July 2017 and March 2018, commissioned, with financial support, by the Institute of European Studies, located in Macau. This research was written up as a paper that took as its title 'Memory and Identity: Macanese Cuisine in the Diaspora'. The research was partly born out of the fact that more Macanese live outside Macau than within, and implicit were concerns about the future of facets of Macanese culture, here specifically the cuisine.

Central to the research process were the unpacking of terms such as 'memory', 'identity', and 'cuisine'; and even an investigation of the nature of 'diaspora' itself. These terms are all also explored here. However, what emerged as a central issue to the discussion about the status of the cuisine was the very definition of Macanese cuisine itself. It became clear that this cuisine cannot be seen in isolation, as a unique product of Portuguese colonialism in the south of China, but needs to be placed in the context of a far broader picture embracing that embraces in particular the cooking styles and techniques (and ingredients) of Goa and Malacca. These port cities also served as Portuguese outposts in Asia. Further, it became clear that Macanese cuisine cannot to be seen viewed solely in the context of Portuguese culinary influence, but has to be seen as part of a group of other, possibly hybrid, cuisines within Asia, and as part of various intra-Asian culinary conversations. Lastly, it cannot be assumed that such culinary conversations have taken place chronologically according to the sequence of Portuguese landings. Rather, a dynamic forum across time and geography is suggested.

The place of food in cultural studies

Critics have gone so far as to say that Marcel Proust changed perceptions of the relevance and importance of the sensory world upon publication of *Remembrance of Things Past*. In placing the aroma and taste memories of the madeleine as a pivotal moment in the search for truth, he seminally privileges the sensory alongside the cerebral; and perhaps even opened the door for food studies. The possible discrepancy in his text between external appearance and corporeal sensory reaction should be stressed. 'Not until he actually tasted the cookie dipped in tea could he fix the gustatory experience and connect it to his life' (Parkhurst Ferguson 2004, 18). On the other hand, to take a couple of examples from poetry, when William Carlos Williams writes of plums in his poem *This Is Just To Say*, they exist as no more than metaphor (of something presumed sexual); and in T. S. Eliot's *The Love Song of J. Alfred Prufrock* a life measured out with coffee spoons speaks metaphorically of routine, boredom, and regret, and not a gustatory pleasure upon waking.

Food anthropologist David Sutton argues that the tendency for the field of food studies to have been considered 'scholarship-lite' may be, at least as far as the field of anthropology is concerned, because 'unlike other cultural domains, such as kinship, ritual and religion, exchange or politics, food does not have its own well-developed specialist terminology and tools of analysis' (Sutton 2001, 3). He presented a paper on the subject of food and memory in 1996 at the Department of Anthropology at Oxford, whereupon the response of an Oxford don was: 'Food and memory? Why would anyone want to remember anything they had eaten?' (Sutton 2001, 1). Though, given the compromise of typical food delivery in the United Kingdom, even as recently as the early 1990s, this comment could be taken rather literally.

It is perhaps the everydayness of food and eating—everyone has to eat, across cultures, across continents (though basic access to sufficient food is here assumed)—which has tended to send it 'back-of-house', as it were. Yet the other two great cultural indicators of culture, religion and language, similarly inform the everyday. As Sutton further argues regarding food, 'this obviousness can be deceptive as well, because food can hide powerful meanings and structures under the cloak of the mundane and the quotidian' (Sutton 2001, 3).

Food studies within the social sciences and history take many forms, of course. Food studies is 'an intrinsically multi-dimensional subject—with social, psychological, physiological, symbolic dimensions, to name merely a few' (Holtzman 2006, 362). We can begin with hunters and gatherers, and how the discovery of fire transformed lifestyles, as well as diets. Industrialisation, as well as the Agricultural Revolution, changed the way we perceive food, and had significant impacts on diet/s. Food taboos, food security, food safety, food sustainability, and food ethics are all powerful markers. Also for important consideration are the social (or other) notions of eating, since eating is almost universally regarded as a sharing process. We can ask apparently simple questions about what we eat and why, whom we eat with,

> at what time, and investigate the 'grammar' of a meal and meal time, and yet in the process emerge with powerful cultural indicators.

Background

Portuguese cooking is embodied on the South China coast in the cuisine of the Macanese. For almost 500 years Portuguese practices and philosophies around food have been in dynamic dialogue with those of Asian cultures. Some intra-Asian culinary conversations have been noted, such as the Nyonya-and-Baba cooking of Malacca (essentially a conversation between Fukien-Chinese and indigenous Malaccan foodways), but the interaction of Portugal with foodways in, particularly, Goa and Malacca, resulted in the creation of a unique cuisine in a third space: Macau. This cuisine is the Macanese cuisine, the food of the Macanese people, who are descendants of the Portuguese, and who consider themselves the 'sons' of the land of Macau.

Who Are the Macanese?

I once asked Macau restaurateur Isabel Eusebio what the Macanese 'look like' and her reply was: '*We* know who we are.' I know she wasn't being dismissive, as she was the first Macanese to urge me, in the early 1990s when I was working as a freelance journalist, to begin to record Macanese culture and in particular the recipes. But it was an answer tinged, I think, with ambivalence.

Yet the first challenge in doing research about an aspect of Macanese culture is to define what it is, and what it means, to be Macanese. We explore in these pages the history of the Macanese people, and the examination of the cuisine helps to piece that history together. There are many questions. To be Macanese do you need to have a male ancestor who would have identified as Portuguese and thereafter various female ancestors from different Asian ethnic groups? If you are the adoptive child of Macanese parents but don't have Macanese blood as such, are you Macanese? Here we are being mindful of those who identify as Macanese—and there may be some (technically) Macanese who don't identify as Macanese. We could also identify a second wave of Macanese, the neo-Macanese, who are the Macau-born progeny of a Portuguese father and a Chinese mother, say, who might well identify as Macanese. There is much to suggest that the Macanese themselves have shifted their identities across time; see, for example, the work of João de Pina-Cabral in *Between China and Europe: Person, Culture and Emotion in Macao* (2002).

There is no government census in Macau to give a definitive answer to the question as to how many Macanese live in Macau—figures such as 10,000 are bandied about—but it is broadly accepted or assumed that those in the Macanese diaspora outnumber those who live in Macau. We have nuanced categories here, too, such as those who were born in the diaspora but have taken up residence in Macau. It could also be noted here that the (ethnically) Portuguese community itself is never deemed to have comprised more than about 7,000, in a territory which now has a population of about 650,000, almost all of which is ethnically Chinese.[1]

Macau and the Macanese

In recent decades, political upheavals and social and cultural changes have led to the perception of an unstable Macau, and identities have become undermined. As sociologist Stuart Hall points out, quoting cultural critic Kobena Mercer, 'identity only becomes an issue when it is in crisis, when something assumed to be fixed, coherent and stable is displaced by the experience of doubt and uncertainty' (Hall 1992, 275).

Such uncertainty became particularly evident in the years leading up to the return of Macau to China in 1999, when many Macanese left Macau. Over a number of decades the diaspora had been moving to Portugal and Portuguese-speaking Brazil, but this newer wave was targeting English-language speaking countries: the United States, Canada, and Australia. Many Portuguese also left prior to or at the moment of the handover, their absence creating additional social and societal change. Recent years, however, in response, have seen a resurgence in the number of young Portuguese arriving in Macau (as well as settling in Hong Kong) to work in the private sector—in response to various European economic crises and Asian opportunities. Their attitude, however, tends to be Eurocentric in approach as opposed to assuming the China/Macau-global identities of the Macanese.

The Macanese Diaspora

When more of a people live outside their community than within, as is the case for the Macanese, what kind of impact might this have on their cuisine, either literally and figuratively, or both? An important element of the research deployed in the preparation for this book was the examination of the relationship that members of the Diaspora have with their own cuisine. It was research that began in 2012, in preparation for a paper that I was to present at a conference on intangible cultural heritage, co-organised by the Chinese University of Hong Kong in January 2013.[2] Or perhaps it had begun before that, when I was researching my 2003 culture-cookbook *Taste of Macau: Portuguese Cuisine on the China Coast*, having first begun to publish on Macau culinary culture with my first book in 1994, entitled, appropriately enough, *Macau on a Plate*.

Macanese Food: At Home in Macau?

This research has been set against the backdrop of a dynamic Macau landscape. It has investigated the status of Macanese food in contemporary Macau; its representation, transformation, commodification, and consumption as part of the tourism package; and how the increasingly cosmopolitan Macanese residents in Macau relate to their own traditional cooking. The research findings compare attitudes towards Macanese food at home and among the diaspora; and the extent to which attitudes to food occupy a dynamic forum within the various and ongoing interactions between Asia and Europe, as well as further afield.

The Role of Diasporic Studies

Research into the migrant's relationship with food has tended to talk of the economic migrant.[3] However, in the 1977 diasporic study entitled *Between Two Cultures: Migrants and Minorities in Britain*, editor James Watson remarks that a unique feature of the collection was that contributors had looked at *both ends* of the migration chain. Indeed, Watson argues that it is impossible to fully understand immigration as a process without investigating families (and kinship) from both sides (Watson 1977, 2). Thus, although many studies have been conducted relating to the migrant and his/her food, for example, Watson's outlook is prescient because it relates to my own study in referencing those Macanese living away from Macau, while simultaneously looking at the (changing) nature of the very place they have left and their relationship to it.

In his own study of the Man Clan from villages in Hong Kong's New Territories, Watson shows how adverse economic conditions at home in the 1950s led to a migration stream to London. Migrants began to open restaurants, paving the way for the formation of the city's Chinatown just off Leicester Square in the West End. The first incumbents of this ghetto were former rice farmers who had become the victims of cheap imported rice from South East Asia, particularly Thailand, which had rendered Hong Kong rice cultivation uncompetitive. In a pattern known as chain migration, brothers sent for cousins, then for nephews and for sons. Those entrepreneurial sons in turn opened their own restaurants, as the central London hub, adjacent to the theatre district, flourished. Meanwhile, changing socio-economic circumstances meant that just as it was becoming too expensive to open a new restaurant because of rising rents, young men were now sending for their wives and children. And so the take-out restaurant was created: a perfect ground-floor business model with accommodation upstairs; and with no labour costs incurred since the family members were harnessed to help out. Any sense of community was now under threat, however, as in order to earn a good living a take-out restaurant had to be some miles (3 miles has been suggested) from the next. Meanwhile, conditions at home in the New Territories were changing, and indeed villages were positively prospering, thanks to remittances.

This sort of chain migration framework, first acknowledging and then addressed through the analysis of changing situations in the homeland as a result of diaspora, is used by Robin Palmer in his explanations of the push-pull factors at play among Italian immigrants from Emilia-Romagna in London (Palmer 1977, 242–68). Palmer demonstrates how they were adaptive to a reasonable extent, particularly because of their ability to exploit certain English agricultural circumstances. For example, 'some purchase pigs in the countryside and form salami-making cooperatives [in London]; whole families go on mushrooming expeditions in the New Forest; and the men rent "shoots"' (Palmer 1977, 250). They also exploited the emerging English taste for Italian food; but were simultaneously able to maintain their *paesani* (Italian-ness), particularly through the establishment of an association that both brought them together as a community and at the same time validated their links with their homeland. Parallels may well be drawn here with the Macanese Casa movement, presented in Appendix 2, and its importance in maintaining Macanese-ness.

In Verity Saifullah Khan's research into Pakistani immigrants in the United Kingdom, she reaches the conclusion that although the relationship between host country and home country would change in subsequent generations, the link was at this point strong. 'Present trends suggest that ties with the homeland and distinctive cultural patterns will remain crucial for many years' (Saifullah Khan 1977, 87).

By asking respondents to share their age in our survey, we seek to ascertain the extent to which this generational difference may be true in the Macanese diaspora, specifically in the way that Macanese of different ages feel about Macau *the place*. But we may also need to consider differing extents of acculturation, which in themselves may have to do with, as an example, the prevalent language spoken in the host country or at home. For example, author Tony da Silva writes not in Portuguese but in English, and one of the reasons for this is because: 'Most Macaenses read English—even those in Portugal and Brazil—but outside of those two countries, they only speak and read English' (personal correspondence, January 2018).

As was shown above, in the case of villages within Hong Kong's New Territories, the extent to which the motherland is transformed by the process and results of emigration should also be factored in. Macau, the place, has not been materially affected by remittances, as the Hong Kong New Territories have been in relation to the London Chinatown model. However, it is being transformed on an almost daily basis, with tourist numbers now approaching 30 million per year against a population of some 650,000. Additionally, many Macanese in the diaspora left because they already felt that they had 'lost' Macau; and that today, the nature of a Macau existing in memory is shown to be markedly different to its contemporary incarnation.

> 'I was there on a short business trip and so much has changed that I don't feel it's the Macau I use to enjoy visiting anymore.' Vitor Souza (personal correspondence, November 2017)

However, the Macanese diasporic movement is not, as each of the three studies mentioned above have in common, critically an economic process. Some Macanese may have moved overseas for education or for professional opportunities; but most have left for social and cultural reasons, and even political reasons (even as some have anecdotally regretted that decision). But the volition has not been to send remittances home. In Macau, economic change and development in the home region are almost exclusively brought about as a result of government initiatives to improve the economy. A further contrast to note is that it was from the early 2000s onwards that the economy was such that Macanese (or anyone who had been born in Macau, of course) were now the first generation to have the option to return to Macau to pursue their careers after education, or who were not required to leave in the first place for employment. The large number of Macau-born people involved at quite senior levels in the hospitality industry, for example, attests to this.

Macau and Food Memories

But the focus of this book is the role of food in terms of identity formation and affirmation, while simultaneously looking at the role of memory in food production, reproduction and consumption.

Marina de Senna Fernandes, a Macau-born Macanese from a prominent family, who relocated to Lisbon and then returned to Macau, has previously shared with me many memories about food in her Macau-based childhood. She told me that she and her friends would, on the walk home from school, try to guess the nationality (Portuguese, Macanese, or Chinese) of the residents of a particular house, based on the aromas emanating from the kitchen. She also talked of the distinctive aromas that would permeate the neighbourhood when her grandmother made Sarrabulho (a Macanese dish based on chicken offal and pig's blood). As a member of the diaspora in Lisbon, she tried to replicate this dish based on smell memory. '[I] am glad to say that I succeeded, but it took me almost five hours in the kitchen to achieve the correct aroma and taste' (Jackson 2003, 28). These comments clearly show how food is memorable from a sensory point of view, in addition to having important commensality (eating together) functions.

I was also struck, some years back, by an opinion expressed by Ed Rozario, a Macanese who has lived in Australia since 1985, regarding the iconic Macanese dish African Chicken. 'Sadly with age the memory can play tricks on the taste buds. One example is the search for Angelo's African Chicken. Within our community around the world, there are legions of amateur cooks experimenting with various ingredients

Figure 0.1: Marina de Senna Fernandes as a child in Macau. Photo courtesy of Marina de Senna Fernandes.

to replicate this famous dish. Funnily, with the passage of time, if we were presented today with a chicken cooked by Angelo himself, we might not recognise it' (personal correspondence, 2012).

One basis, then, of this research was to discover the extent to which Macanese cuisine is important as a thread of cultural identity, but also to investigate the role of memory in attitudes to Macanese cooking as opposed to, or alongside, physical engagement in its preparation. I wanted to examine factors that might create a plurality of attitudes to Macanese cuisine, including access or otherwise to the necessary ingredients, the propensity for interaction with other Macanese, and marriage patterns based on ethnicity.

Food and Memory

How might we work towards a definition of memory around food, and how do we remember food? Is it through aroma? Or can we remember food first through remembering the people with whom we shared it, or the place in which we consumed it? Does the eating of Macanese food transplant a Macanese living outside Macau back to a family home on Rua Central; or perhaps to Restaurante Solmar?

In his research paper 'Food and Memory', which appeared in *The Annual Review of Anthropology* in 2006, anthropologist Jon Holtzman outlines his own interest in the broader phenomenon of memory, seeing it as a multilayered and multidimensional subject 'with social, psychological, physiological, symbolic dimensions . . . and with culturally constructed meanings' (Holtzman 2006, 362). He looks at ways in which the present is informed by the past through memory, talking of 'the subjective ways that the past is recalled, memorialized, and used to construct the present' (Holtzman 2006, 363).

Figure 0.2: Family visit to the grandparents' former Macau home on Rua Tap Seac. Photo courtesy of Mac Gutierrez.

Another important point he raises is how food and memory are sensually linked (taste, aroma) and yet how something as apparently personal as the eating act is also called upon to traverse public domains. 'Unlike our other most private activities, food is integrally constituted through its open sharing, whether in rituals, feasts, reciprocal exchange, or contexts in which it is bought and sold' (Holtzman 2006, 373). This raises the question of the relative importance of collectively shared culinary memories versus or in conjunction with one's own personal memories, thus talking directly to the question of identity.

In his 1914 ethnographic monographs of the Trobriand Islanders (these islands form part of Papua New Guinea), the influential anthropologist Bronisław Malinowksi noted that this matriarchal society located memory not in the brain but in the stomach. This belief adds an interesting footnote, underlying which is the assumption of a core link between memory and the consumption of food. So not only are we what we *eat*, after Brillat-Savarin, but 'we are what we *ate* as well' (Sutton 2001, 7) (my italic).

There are two important full-length works in food studies where memory is held to be a core reference point, and both are cited by Holtzman. First is David Sutton's *Remembrance of Repasts: An Anthropology of Food and Memory* (2001)—the title presumably being a play on the Proust title (though the most recent translation of this book, 2003, is entitled *In Search of Lost Time*). This book is a study of the residents of the Greek island of Kalymnos. The second is Carole Counihan's *Around the Tuscan Table: Food, Family, and Gender in Twentieth-Century Florence* (2004).

Counihan, an anthropologist with a particular interest in feminism, began her research in Florence within an extended family, with a gender-based trajectory. However, she found that among her informants gender was so glaringly and specifically central in foodways that she shifted her focus to cuisine: 'The division of labour around food revealed gender roles and relations.' She found that the entry of more women to the workforce, and the absence of gender parity at home in the realms of housework and cooking, were critical challenges to the preservation of traditional food preparation and diet, and with broader implications too: 'Their foodways expressed values and habits central to their lives' (Counihan 2004, 1). Thus: 'As foodways change, so does the culture' (Counihan 2004, 191); and she links this discourse with memory and nostalgia.

Implicit in any study of memory is the process or act of forgetting—whether conscious or unconscious. We might choose to forget, for example, periods when we were required to eat food we did not like or which we did not consider food (for example, a meal is not a meal unless it contains a pasta course or finishes with rice); or when there was simply not enough food. On the other hand, times when there was a shortage of food, such as during wartime, might alternatively become tinged or even framed by nostalgia: Counihan describes how her Tuscan informants frame their food thoughts around the idea that in the past there may have been little to eat but it tasted good: *poco, ma buono*, as opposed to there being plenty to eat in the present, but that its qualities may be called into question: *molto, ma buono*. 'Today, if you eat, let's say spinach, or Swiss chard, or beet greens—everything tastes the same. But in the old days, if you ate spinach, it had a distinct flavour,' explained an elderly member of the family (Counihan 2004, 179). A subsequent question we might ask, then, is not only as to whether Macanese food tasted better in the past—but does it also taste better in Macau?

Various examples of how memory might operate around food are explored by David Sutton in *Remembrance of Repasts: An Anthropology of Food and Memory*. The idea of a link between remembering food and preparing food is mooted: 'One of the main threats to food memories... is lack of knowledge of food production' (Sutton 2001, 165). In the preface, he recalls his own childhood repasts. Guests were frequently entertained around his parents' dining table, and he writes that if his parents asked if he remembered Mr. So-and-So, he would ask what they were eating for dinner when that particular guest visited, and only after recalling the meal would he be able to picture the person referred to (Sutton 2001, x).

Sutton also explores how seasonal food cycles are concerned with 'prospective memory'—we could take as examples the shared, animated anticipation (connected powerfully with positive memories of the last one) of, say, Yunnan Province's wild mushroom season; or the water melon season in Beijing, when carts are piled high with fruit; or Lunar New Year (known as Tet) celebrations in Vietnam, as Nir Avieli's observation recorded in *Rice Talks: Food and Community in a Vietnamese Town* decidedly illustrates: 'My Hoianese friends were discussing Tet, planning it, and eagerly awaiting its arrival from the moment I arrived in town in 1999, four months before the holiday; they frequently reminisced about the Tet festivities that year until the Mid-Autumn Festival, some eight months after the new year, when preparations for the coming Tet began. "Will you come for Tet?" is the question most often asked by my Vietnamese friends' (Avieli 2012, 200). He shows how an invitation to join Tet celebrations translates as 'eat Tet'; and that while many traditions central to Tet are gradually disappearing, 'the dishes prepared for Tet are extremely popular and play a significant role' (Avieli 2012, 201). He further comments how the act of celebrating ('eating') new year with family was a critical part of Vietnamese identity, and even humanity itself; and this centrality to self can equally be applied to, for example, David Sutton's Greek island.

'The food event evokes a whole world of family, agricultural associations, place names and other "local knowledge"' (Sutton 2001, 83). On Kalymnos, he even found that memories of local water sources shared all of these evocations, because waters sourced from different places were used for different purposes—for example, water from one spot was used for the soaking of beans; water from a different source was used for the watering of olive trees. Sutton looks at how the act of sharing food links a diner to the others at the table, how it links back through memory to previous meals, and indeed, through its repetition, links to previous generations.

Sutton shows how aromas may take on deep symbolism and how smell can evoke deep emotion. Basil is not used extensively in Greek cooking, as compared with, say,

Italy. However, basil-infused water forms part of the Greek bread-making process. A Greek student studying in London, on seeing a pot of basil, wistfully reported how '[i]t really smells like Greece.' Such a statement is suggestive of 'the importance of the sensory in reconnecting and remembering experiences and places one has left behind'. Further, the process of basil being newly, and individually, taken as a national symbol of Greece, 'suggests that objects can shift levels of identity when experienced in new contexts' (Sutton 2001, 74).

This research introduces an additional element, as compared with Sutton's work in *Remembrance of Repasts*, and that is the state of Macanese food in contemporary Macau, and how cross-generational memories of, and attitudes to, Macanese cuisine at home might vary as compared to those of the diaspora. This research also examines how the very status of Macanese food within Macau may have changed over time. It addresses the idea that a cuisine is not fixed in time; but nor is it contained within a single history: the cuisine may have seen transformations not only among the diaspora, but at home too.

Cuisine or Cooking?

Implicit in this research the attempt to discover when and if Macanese food became a 'cuisine' rather than simply being what Macanese cooked and consumed on a daily (or more or less daily) basis. Is there even such a thing as a cuisine on a national level? A historical distinction between the cooking of the elite and the food of the other is noted—the haute cuisine of the French, for example, and Imperial cuisine in a China context. There is, however, a further and important distinction that can be made—which concerns on the one hand the habitual,[4] and on the other performance.

This leads to the discourse about what a cuisine is, who is awarded the privilege of defining a cuisine, and what purpose that cuisine might serve. That Macanese cuisine will have an entry (written by this author) in the *Berkshire Encyclopedia of Chinese Cuisines*, a five-volume work to be published in cooperation with Oxford University Press (2020) indicates that 'history' has recognised it as a legitimate culinary contribution in the Chinese context. But is it recognised, and to what extent, within Macau? Ergo, should it perhaps have a palpable presence on the pages of, for example, Portuguese cookbooks?

The definition of cuisine, in a dictionary sense, would probably run something like this: A style or method of cooking, especially as characteristic of a particular country, region, or establishment; or food cooked in a certain way. To this we might add provisions such as a requirement for there to be a coherent group of dishes that together form a cuisine.

In his research paper 'Food and the Counterculture', Warren Belasco sets about defining cuisine, and does it thus: as a 'set of socially situated food behaviours with these components: a limited number of edible foods (selectivity), a preference for a particular way of preparing foods (technique); a distinctive set of flavour, textural and visual characteristics (aesthetics); a set of rules for consuming food (infrastructure). Embedded in these components are a set of ideas, images, and values (ideology) that can be "read" just like any other cultural "text"' (Belasco 2005, 219–20).

Ideas contained here, such as 'limited number'; 'particular way of preparing', and 'set of flavour . . . characteristics' do not immediately appear to apply to Macanese food, given its extraordinary breadth in terms of food stuffs, preparation methods, and its refusal to be confined to the 'sweet-salty' or 'salty-sour' type of dialectic. Does Macanese cuisine have its own unique set or parameters? Does something 'thrown together' in the domestic kitchen—as Macanese cooking is often represented—constitute a cuisine in the rigid definitional sense?

The food moniker 'fusion' did little to progress the study of the nature of cuisine.[5] Macanese cooking has sometimes been labelled the world's first fusion cooking, and that assertion may contain some truth in the sense that it juxtaposed ingredients that had likely never seen each other: soy sauce and bay leaf, for example. But fusion implies that you're fusing something concrete to something concrete, which is not the case with Macanese food. Portuguese cuisine may have originally been the foundation of Macanese cuisine—though represented in a third space, many miles from the motherland—but here we have the cooking styles, ingredients, and traditions of multiple cultures coming together to create something entirely new.[6] This process is distinct from hybridity, which refers to a process that results in the changing of culinary traditions and habits within a single culture. Fusion food, as represented in the public domain, is an entirely conscious creative act of (re)production; it is something performed.

Are these distinctions between fusion, creolisation, hybridity, and cuisine in a 'pure' sense important within culinary discourse? Certainly they can help us to explore cuisines that are neither linear nor geographically delimited, and may not fit neatly into a class- or status-driven matrix of high and low cooking.

Is Macanese cooking a cuisine? In response to the latter question, Zhang Yang and Pang Ching Lin argue that, in terms of the drawing of a distinction between its place of origin and its reinvention, 'Macanese cuisine has become . . . a full-fledged cuisine, evolving from home food enjoyed at home to a home food cuisine offered in restaurants' (Zhang and Pang 2012, 935). But further distinctions are required here, the first of which is concerned with the significant gap between the daily, domestic culinary practices of the Macanese and those practices that enter the public arena by way of clubs and restaurants; or the inclusion of a few Macanese dishes on pan-Asian, all-day-dining restaurant menus. Cuisines can be, and are, 'used' as part of the tourism package, wherein a fight for authenticity emerges. The removal of pork from dishes on menus in Chinese and Nyonya restaurants in Malaysia is one example; the appropriation of Macanese dishes in Cantonese restaurants in Macau is another. Both these practices will be explored further within these pages.

Summation of Chapters

Chapters 1, 2, and 3 deal directly with the SurveyMonkey findings, relating to cultural identity around food among the diaspora and at home in Macau, and all the time in the context of a changing Macau.

Chapter 1 specifically seeks to explore the relationship between the act of cooking Macanese food, the act of consuming Macanese food, the frequency of such consumption, and its importance in terms of being Macanese. Explored in detail are the shared views of the Macanese community in Hong Kong, in contrast to the rest of the diaspora, for there may emerge some significant differences, with regard to community, beyond Macau, and beyond even family. The symbolism of eating Macanese food, as a way of relating to Macau the place, as opposed to simply eating Macanese food, is also investigated.

Chapter 2 looks at the history of the restaurant scene in Macau, which, it is argued, has probably only existed since the 1980s except for a few higher-end hotel restaurants; though definitely of importance were clubs and the dining rooms at, for example, police headquarters. Explored thereafter is the question of the visibility of Macanese food within Macau, and whether it is by definition a food of the home, rather than one of the foodways in the public domain. The impact of tourism in Macau on traditional foodways is also explored. The difficulties of defining Macanese cuisine within the dominant Cantonese food offering, and the historic Portuguese definitions, also relate to how Macanese food is perceived in the broader population.

Chapter 3 addresses head on the idea that it is asserted that Macanese cuisine is disappearing, but places this assertion in the context that this phenomena of loss might relate to the cultural habits of the Macanese themselves. The importance of family, and beyond that generations of ancestors, is explored. Examined is the nature of the cookbook, and the meaning of the preservation of the recipe in the first place.

Chapter 4 sets the scene for the importance of considering Macanese cuisine not only as a unique cultural artefact, but as a cuisine that must be considered within the broader context of Portuguese culinary influence in Asia. This relates significantly to both the Columbian Exchange and the spice trade, which also had global connotations in terms of changing agricultural practices and eating habits. It also relates to the specific culinary conversations into which the Portuguese entered in Asia, and how those Occidental–Oriental conversations might relate to intra-Asian culinary conversations. This might even take the shape of a single ingredient, such as a fermented or preserved fish sauce. The central role of religion in culinary practice, as well as conversation, is also considered.

Chapter 5 relates, against the ephemeral backdrop of the significant lack of recorded history, specifically how Macanese cuisine might have evolved in the kitchen and how it might thus be defined in a broad cultural arena. It takes specific dishes as examples (Minchi, African Chicken, the condiment Balichão) and also compares Macanese dishes to, for example, Kristang dishes—the foodways of Portuguese descendants in Malacca. It also explores how the cuisine might have interacted with the Chinese community, most particularly regarding the so-called Merenda Man, but also in the politicised, linguistic arena in contemporary Macau, officially part of China since 1999.

1

Macanese Food and Cultural Identity

Macanese cuisine sits within the very narrow band of cuisines that are *so* tightly, *so* decisively, bound up with notions of identity. As a cuisine, it falls firmly in the cultural sphere, but also resonates viscerally. In other national cuisines, such as Italian or Chinese, we see regional differences, such as the use of butter rather than olive oil, or between someone who might be defined as a bread eater rather than a rice eater. Elsewhere, defining someone as a cabbage eater rather than a meat eater is highly likely to be disparaging. In national cuisines, such as Italian or French, we might make factual regional differentiations regarding the use of butter rather than olive oil. In Chinese cuisine, to distinguish between a rice eater and a bread eater, might possibly belie a value judgement. Historically, in Europe, to distinguish between someone who was a cabbage or potato eater as compared to a meat eater was almost certainly a racist slur, indicative of social standing, too.

But the make-up of your mixed ethnic ancestry is probably seldom as glaringly apparent as it is on the plate of food, or selection of sharing dishes, in front of you, as it is with the Macanese. The daily consumption of pasta might unconsciously remind you on a daily basis that you are Italian (at least Italian with a keen sense of your particular region, or your particular type of pasta or sauce). Similarly, the daily consumption of Minchi might unconsciously reaffirm your Macanese identity on a daily basis. But what is it to be Macanese, or what *was* it to be Macanese, and how might that now be different—both for yourself, but most particularly for the Other, or a range of Others?

> 'It [Macanese food] is an important part of my childhood and sense of heritage.'
> —Survey respondent

> 'I enjoyed it [Macanese food] all my life and it is part of my identity.' —Survey respondent

Macanese foodways are based on locally available ingredients, as are most bodies of recipes that might be deemed to be a cuisine, but they also incorporate ingredients from beyond that are similarly readily available owing to factors such as trade and climate. As explored in Chapter 5, which seeks to define Macanese cuisine, even the name of a dish, let alone the actual ingredients, talks deeply of the Macanese people and their miscegenation. It is one of those cuisines—and one might think here of

Peranakan cooking in Malaysia or the Creole cooking of New Orleans—where the juxtaposition of eating habits and culinary traditions from at least two, but possibly multiple, cultures results in the birth of a new foodway.

Research methodology is outlined in Appendix 1, but the reason for asking survey respondents an apparently highly generic question such as where they live was to try to establish if patterns emerged regarding attitudes to Macanese food according to factors such as geographical location, dominant language/s, dominant host country cuisine/s and so on, with regard to cultural identity. The attitudes and comments of diaspora respondents were then compared with those of Macanese living in Macau. I believed that Macanese expatriates living in Hong Kong could potentially have a different—perhaps stronger?—sense of Macanese-ness given their proximity to Macau; and so it is in Hong Kong that we start our culinary and cultural analysis.

The Macanese Community of Hong Kong

I had been pondering whether the sense of Macanese-ness—in this case measured through Macanese food, this being one of the few remaining cultural traits with importance and visibility—would be stronger because of Macau being a mere hour away across the water. Additionally, the Hong Kong environment has traditionally shared many characteristics with Macau, such as Cantonese being the dominant language/dialect and the produce for sale in wet markets being very similar and thus familiar, to take just two everyday examples.

The first striking realisation that the situation is more nuanced than this came when I asked Macanese residents of Hong Kong how often they travel to Macau. Responses suggest in general a high level of engagement with Macanese cuisine both in terms of cultural identity and in literal consumption, with half reportedly eating Macanese food weekly, or even daily. Only one respondent reported that he never eats Macanese, or at least never cooks it. This respondent was in possession of his great-grandmother's recipes, but he reported insufficient spare time to cook such time-consuming dishes. Most members of this Hong Kong community freely share recipes and believe that they should be shared—'the more, the better' responded one, emphatically. But when we mention Macau, rather than Macanese food, it is apparent that there is little engagement with Macau itself: with Macau the motherland, with Macau the place. The vast majority reported that they visited Macau annually or occasionally. One reported that he *never* goes to Macau. Why might that be? Other responses are shown here:

> 'I go when I have to . . . apart from the Macau Grand Prix and other sporting events, [I] hardly go there.' —Survey respondent

> 'Have not been there for the past 10 years. There is no particular reason for going there as all my friends are here in Hong Kong.' —Respondent (personal correspondence, November 2017)

'My parents are from Macau but I was born in Hong Kong and since my father passed away when I was 5, I wasn't exposed to my roots or connected to Macau.' —Simon Ramos (personal correspondence, November 2017)

These findings are of little surprise to Patrick Rozario, with whom I conducted a telephone conversation in January 2018. He is the president of Club Lusitano in Hong Kong (and he is also treasurer of Club de Recreio in Hong Kong; and a member of the Casa in Toronto, where his father and other family members live). The more prominent Macanese families have a history in Hong Kong dating back to the 1800s, he explained. Others moved to Hong Kong after the war in search of work but, following the riots of the 1960s and 1970s and then the impending Handovers of Hong Kong and Macau, left for North America. This being the case, Macanese living in Hong Kong today probably only have distant family members in Macau, so don't feel particularly connected to the Macanese community within Macau.

Some Macanese families have reported that sections of the family left for Shanghai while others left for Hong Kong, and the sense of community between those living in these two cities—in other words beyond Macau but seminally in the same part of the world—is also apparent from the Anthology circulating in those groups beyond Macau, and believed to be have been produced and edited in Shanghai. In this Anthology, Macau the place was not part of the cultural identity 'puzzle' (see also Chapters 3 and 5). This perception contrasts with that of many members of the broader diaspora, for whom, based on their survey responses, a real or imagined Macau resides whether in their memory, in their identity, or in their soul.

This strong connection of Macanese born in Hong Kong to the place/space of Hong Kong also indicates that the Hong Kong Macanese community is relatively self-assured. This is quite likely attributable to its long history and its two long-established clubs—Club Lusitano in Central, which dates from 1866, and Club de Recreio in Kowloon, which dates from 1906. Club de Recreio, established as and continuing as a sports club, retains some of its Portuguese identity, and its officers continue to be Macanese, according to Rozario, even while most of the members are Chinese. Meanwhile, Club Lusitano has been required to make changes. Membership, which had shrunk to an unsustainable 170, is now standing at 270, with a drive to grow to 500. It is now more diverse, including a few young Portuguese expatriates living and working in Hong Kong, with their more European outlook; Chinese with Portuguese nationality; Brazilians with dual nationality; and even a Shanghai Jewish family with Portuguese ancestry.

The a la carte menu currently consists of Macanese and Portuguese dishes, but Rozario believes it will become increasingly Portuguese. Portuguese food, he believes, is more suited to business lunches, while Macanese is more family-style, more leisurely. French and Californian wines are now included alongside the 200 Portuguese labels. Rozario explains that he sees the need for links to the past, but also a need to look to the future.

Further, we can see that the Macanese community in Hong Kong even took aspects of what was regarded as Macanese cuisine, or the foods eaten by the Macanese, in a more Hong Kong—read British—direction, and not only with the iconic Minchi (see Chapter 5 for a description and analysis of this dish). British influence can be seen in some of the Macanese culinary traditions at Christmas, particularly in baked cakes made with dried fruit; in the substitution of sherry for port; in the popular addition of Lea & Perrins Worcestershire Sauce to various dishes including curry (see, for example, Jorge da Silva 2016, 154); and in a dish as 'humble' as Cheese Toasts, with which most British children living as expats in Hong Kong would have been familiar at tea time. We now compare recipes for a classic British (Welsh!) rendering of the dish, to one that originated in the Portuguese community in Hong Kong.

Welsh Rarebit

This is an adaptation of Welsh Rarebit (or Rabbit, depending on which food historians and writers one aligns with). This dish is essentially cheese melted under the grill on slices of toast but rather more refined than that, with various ingredients added to the Cheddar.

Welsh rarebit

If you think Welsh Rarebit is just cheese on toast, try this . . . served with a crisp British apple, peppery watercress, and a handful of walnuts. Check your Worcestershire Sauce—Lea & Perrins original is not suitable for vegetarians as it includes anchovy. However, there are several that don't and will still give you that savoury kick.

Serves 4
Prep Time: 10 minutes
Cook time: 5 minutes

150 ml beer
1 tbs Worcester sauce
25 g butter
25 g flour
1 tsp dry mustard – optional
150 ml milk
100 g grated strong cheese
4 slices of toast (granary or walnut bread is especially good)

Preheat the grill. Put the beer and Worcester sauce into a small saucepan and boil hard until reduced by half. Melt the butter in a separate pan and mix in the flour and mustard to form a ball (a roux). Mix in the milk gradually and cook, stirring until smooth and thick. Mix in the reduced beer. Stir in the cheese. Divide between the toast slices and pop under the grill until browned and bubbling. Serve immediately.

(Included here with kind permission of Sarah Beattie, and based on a recipe from her father's family in South Wales. This recipe first appeared in her 2014 book, Meat-Free Any Day).

Macanese Cheese Toast

Tony Jorge da Silva includes a recipe for Cheese Toast in his cookbook *Macaense Cuisine* (Jorge da Silva, 2016), a recipe given to him by a Club Lusitano chef in 1997. The addition of a sprinkling of Parmesan on the top was a more recent kitchen innovation (between 2000 and 2005). I've seen this dish served at parties in Macau, for example at Riquexo restaurant. It is truly time-consuming to create it for, say, 100 guests, as it is rather like the potato cubes fried for Minchi—it is necessary to prepare twice as many as you first thought because they tend to go missing! Tony da Silva says that Cheese Toast, and the related Shrimp Toast, may sound and seem very commonplace: I assume by this he means without specific (Macanese) cultural reference. However, for those Macanese who lived in Hong Kong in the 1950s and 1960s, these two toasts would immediately locate them in respectively Club Lusitano and Club de Recreio. Further, 'the term "toast" says they are of British origin, so to name Cheese Toast as Torrada de Queizo would be very strange!' (Tony da Silva, personal correspondence, November 2017).[1] A recipe for Cheese Toast is here reproduced, by kind permission of Tony da Silva.

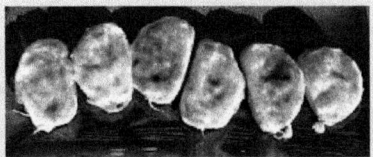

Cheese toast (serves 12)

Lusitano, Hong Kong

Ingredients
6 slices white bread, crust cut off, toasted, and cut into triangular halves; or French baguette, sliced
¾ lb Edam cheese, finely grated
¼ lb Parmesan cheese, grated (optional)
¼ lb unsalted butter, softened

> 3 tsp Coleman's mustard powder
> 2 tsp sugar
> ½ tsp salt
> ½ tsp Lea & Perrins Worcestershire sauce
>
> Method
> 1. Lightly toast the bread slices, then set aside
> 2. Thoroughly mix all other ingredients to the consistency of a thick paste
> 3. Spread the paste, thicker in the middle, on one side of each bread slice
> 4. Place the slices under the low broiler, cheese side up, until the surfaces of the cheese are medium-brown
> 5. Serve right away

How Often Do You Eat Macanese Food?

> 'Most families (myself included) do not cook traditional dishes on a regular basis and the younger generation is not interested in learning how to prepare them.' —Vitor Souza (personal correspondence, November 2017)

I felt this was a companion, or at least supplementary, question to the one about Macanese food and cultural identity. If a cuisine is a strong part of your identity, does that equate to your actually eating it or your cooking it? Were respondents more likely to eat Macanese food if they themselves cooked it? So the next question also seemed important: Who prepares the Macanese food? A further sub-question relates to the relationship between cooking the food you eat or eating food cooked by someone else. Is the food more literally part of you if you have cooked it, and does the link to ancestry thus become (more?) embodied? This area is explored in some detail in Chapter 3, in the section about beliefs around the meanings of recipes. Or is it through the process and act of cooking, and the subsequent eating of the resulting dish, that it becomes part of you? Indeed, one respondent specifically raised this issue.

> 'Since I don't know how to cook, it is not possible for me to furnish exactly my relationship with macanese [sic] food. But, as a 100% macanese [sic], I enjoy and appreciate it.' —Survey respondent

There are multiple indications that Macanese food, except within Macau, is moving away from being 'every day' food to something more symbolic and ceremonial. It can still be enjoyed, but perhaps just once a year, in the context of a large, seasonal gathering, perhaps around Christmas.

> 'It's what I grew up eating but I don't prepare it at home.' —Survey respondent

> 'It is traditional food, particularly for the Christmas cooking and family gathering.' —Survey respondent

It doesn't necessarily have to be eaten daily to remain an important part of cultural identity. With the exclusion of data from Hong Kong and Macau, the number of respondents who rank Macanese cuisine as an important part of their cultural identity is 65 per cent—while only 42 per cent of those eat Macanese food at least weekly. The figures among Hong Kong respondents is reasonably similar.

However, in Macau, 75 per cent of respondents report that Macanese cuisine is an important part of their identity, and 75 per cent of respondents report that they eat it at least on a weekly basis, with nearly half of those eating it on a daily basis. Interesting, the proportion of Macau (and Hong Kong) respondents reporting that they personally cook Macanese food is much lower when compared with the broader diaspora. That Macanese food can be readily found in Macau—whether for a workday lunch or a weekend family dinner, either take-out or eat in—is surely responsible for this phenomenon, as is the restaurant at Club Lusitano in Hong Kong, which is open on a daily basis. Sonia Palmer, owner of Riquexo restaurant in Macau, reports that they have customers who come in every single day—'that's why our menu changes every day'—and when they opened, in 1978, they offered a home delivery service, catering to the same coterie of elderly people every day. 'Nowadays we don't deliver meals anymore. But we do cater for parties' (personal correspondence, January 2018).

Who Prepares the Macanese Food?

There was a clear pattern of results to this question. A total of 150 respondents said that the person doing the cooking was 'me', 'my partner or spouse', or 'another family member'. Just twenty-six responded that when they ate Macanese food, it was prepared by a Macanese person from outside the family. Taking Hong Kong as a separate case, eighteen of the aforementioned twenty-six live in the broader diaspora, and all reported eating Macanese food monthly or annually. Such consumption patterns are certainly indicative of the important role that the Casa movement plays,[2] with its monthly and annual community events that typically include the serving of Macanese food.

Who cooks? This question is problematic, in that people who cook may also eat Macanese food prepared by someone else when eating outside the home. If a respondent says they eat Macanese food on a weekly basis, it may not mean that they cook Macanese food on a weekly basis. Furthermore, we should consider the case of someone who might cook monthly for 100 people, as opposed to weekly for two people. Bearing these caveats in mind, the results indicated that 65 per cent of those who cooked Macanese food ate Macanese food at least weekly, if not daily; and that around 35 per cent ate or cooked it on a monthly basis.

Of those who responded to the question of who cooks as 'Me', the results showed that although respondents ranged in age from twenty-five to seventy-five or over, a small majority was noted in the sixty-five to seventy-four age group. However, the results were highly genderised, with just twenty men saying they cooked, as opposed to fifty-three women.

Figure 1.2: Dinner dance of the Uniao Macaense Americana, 2015. Photo courtesy of Ricardo Collaco.

Macanese Is My Favourite Cuisine

With this statement, to which respondents could mark their response from 'strongly agree' to 'strongly disagree', the bell curve showed that 62 per cent agreed or strongly agreed, while only 7 per cent disagreed. What I wanted to begin to explore was a correlation between the frequency of eating Macanese food and how Macanese cuisine is viewed, and again trace such findings back to the question of the relationship between Macanese food and identity. What was striking were the geographical variations. Of those respondents based in Macau, 75 per cent said it was their favourite food, showing a direct correlation with the percentages of those eating Macanese food regularly and with their strong sense of identity around Macanese food. In the diaspora (not including Hong Kong), 61 per cent said it was their favourite, which was slightly lower than the percentage who said Macanese food was an important part of their identity. In Hong Kong, the number who said it was their favourite was the lowest, at 57 per cent, though, in common with the greater diaspora, was slightly lower than those who expressed the importance of Macanese food for their cultural identity.

Conclusion

Stating that Macanese cuisine is a key part of your cultural identity can be interpreted in the abstract. Macanese cuisine does not have to be your favourite cuisine, you may never cook it yourself, and you may eat it only rarely—but its importance is embedded in identity. This finding exactly mirrors the conclusions reached about the role of national dishes, such as Brazil's Feijoada. In *Rice & Beans: A Unique Dish in a Thousand*

Places it is stated: 'Clearly there is no close connection between how important rice and beans may be in people's minds, and how often they put it in their stomachs' (Wilk and Barbosa 2012).

Macanese cuisine may be seen as something that goes beyond food and beyond calories, because what is clearly very important is who cooks it (usually Mum), whom it is eaten with (family, community, members of a Casa or club), and when it is eaten (Christmas, a christening, a wedding anniversary). It is more than apparent that a representation of a food identity, or just a single dish such as Minchi, may only be literally consumed once a year, yet it is favoured, simultaneously culturally and theoretically, above all other.

Figure 1.3: Jorge family, Macau, 1919. Photo courtesy of the Graça Pacheco Jorge and Pedro Barreiros collection.

2
Macanese Food in Macau

How he missed Macau having left it. He could still feel his friend's warm embrace. He felt a vague need to cry. Two weeks in his homeland after an absence of twenty-four years had hardly been enough. It would have been better if he hadn't come back. But how could a Macanese turn down the chance of seeing his homeland again... He had made full use of his stay. He had satisfied his long craving for Macanese and Chinese food, savoured with their own local ingredients.
—Extract from the short story 'Candy' by Henrique de Senna Fernandes (2002)

Is Macanese food invisible in Macau? Invisible to some, maybe; or to many? Or its existence may not even be known about? Or invisible because it does not actually exist? Where, exactly, does Macanese food sit in physical versus metaphysical or metaphorical

Figure 2.1: Lawyer and novelist Henrique de Senna Fernandes with daughter, Marina de Senna Fernandes, 1970s. Photo courtesy of Marina de Senna Fernandes.

terms? Perhaps it is in the process of disappearing, or on the other hand (but perhaps simultaneously) emerging more strongly but in a transformed state: making the move away from the home kitchen and onto the menus of restaurants in casino hotels. How exactly is Macanese food presented and represented in Macau, we might further ponder. To investigate more deeply how the Macanese diaspora relates to Macanese cuisine, an effective counterbalance is to see how Macanese living in Macau feel about the representation, validity and reputation, or otherwise, of their cuisine at home.

Macanese Food outside Macau

For the Macanese in the diaspora, it is almost impossible to find Macanese restaurants or restaurants serving Macanese dishes. A pop-up Macanese restaurant in London in 2014, run by a highly trained Hong Kong Chinese chef, simply failed to take off, though those who did attend enjoyed the experience immensely. Fat Rice in Chicago bills itself as Macanese, or at least as *inspired* by the Macanese cooking of Macau; and in Malaysia there's a restaurant called Fat Tea Macanese Food, co-owned by a Macanese. In January 2019, Portuguese chef Kei de Freitas is about to open a Macanese restaurant in Edinburgh.

> 'As time goes by and as the older generation passes on, Macanese food is slowly but surely disappearing. Apart from being in Macau, trying to find Macanese food is almost an impossibility unless there are older family members or close friends around or if one has an avid interest and has kept up such interest.' —Survey respondent

Beyond the realm of the restaurant, the ability to cook Macanese food at home is dependent on whether there is a Chinese/Asian provisions store nearby, where items such as Indian tamarind and Cantonese lap cheong can be purchased, though other staples of the Macanese store cupboard, such as soy sauce, bay leaf, and rice noodles, are largely available in mainstream supermarkets.

Is Macanese Food Visible in Macau?

> 'I think Macanese cuisine is widely accepted as a unique and integral part of Macau culture, so I find it surprising that there aren't more restaurants in Macau serving traditional Macanese fare . . . I think most people who try Macanese food enjoy it.' —Johann Almeida (personal correspondence, November 2017)

> 'Honestly in my opinion there are far too few "Macanese" restaurants.' —Luis Lobo, assistant vice-president, Galaxy Entertainment Group (personal correspondence, November 2017)

> 'Things are not good in terms of supply of Macanese food around town. Notwithstanding all the publicity and awareness, something is not working.' — Prominent Macanese resident of Macau

> 'There are excellent restaurants there serving Macanese and Portuguese dishes and I am sure that they are recognised by Macanese living there.' —Survey respondent

> 'There are some restaurants but they are not exclusively Macanese cuisine. You probably need a recommendation from a local.' —Survey respondent

> 'It is no longer the authentic Macanese food I grew up with.' —Survey respondent

Is Macanese food invisible in Macau? This was one of the questions raised by SurveyMonkey. Given a choice between 1 and 5, the majority occupied the middle ground, and thereby 'somewhat agreed' with the statement. Many respondents who had not visited Macau in the recent past understandably refrained from commenting. Of all the people who would know how to find Macanese food in Macau, the most likely are of course the Macanese living in Macau. Members of the diaspora, when visiting Macau for an Encontro,[1] say they eat excellent Macanese food at restaurants selected by local Macanese, as well as enjoying a number of Macanese buffet banquets such as the welcome feast, the Cha Gordo, which would be cooked by members of the Macanese Gastronomy Association in Macau.

In reality there are probably just two 'authentic' Macanese restaurants in Macau, those being Riquexo and APOMAC, though one Macanese whom I interviewed in person in October 2017 questions even their authenticity, for he believes that Macanese cuisine is by definition something cooked in the family home by Macanese. 'These restaurants may be "in essence" Macanese, but production is not completely controlled,' he says, citing as an example cooks who are ethnically Filipino. In any event, these restaurants are away from the parts of town where tourists on foot might find them by accident. To this short list we might add Restaurante Carlos and Dom Galo, in the reclaimed NAPE area. Other ('Portuguese' and, increasingly, 'Cantonese') restaurants serve a number of Macanese dishes, but it may be that in this process of mix-and-match menus one of the problems around perceived visibility of Macanese food arises.

Culinary Definitions

In its propensity to fall somewhat under the radar, the nature of Macanese foodways is not entirely unique,

> 'Macau is such a small speck in the map that most people would never hear about Macanese food at all.' —Francisco Osmund (personal correspondence, January 2018)

It may be relevant here to compare Macanese cuisine to Malaysian cuisine, and while this cuisine is a foodway upon which Macanese draws, there may be some further pertinent similarities regarding perception, availability, and reach. Research has shown that Malaysian cooking does not have the profile of, for example, Indonesian cooking (and perhaps more specifically the terrifically popular Balinese restaurant complete with Hindu iconography). It is considered more 'home-cooked' in style—mirroring Macanese—and it has been argued that this is because consumers don't really understand what it is. A blend of Indian and Chinese, perhaps; or similar to but not as 'good' as Indonesian (Yoshino 2010).

Among Malaysians themselves, those living overseas would, broadly speaking, feel perfectly comfortable in an Indian or (halal) Chinese restaurant (see, for example, Yoshino 2010), in the same way that Macanese feel comfortable eating Chinese and Portuguese—not to mention Italian, Mexican, Vietnamese, and so on, given the breadth of flavours contained with the Macanese canon.

A study undertaken in Japan found that the reason for the lack of provision of, or popularity of, Malaysian restaurants was that consumers 'cannot think of any specific dish. While one can think of tom yam as a representative Thai dish, or raw spring rolls and pho as typically Vietnamese and nasi goreng as something Indonesian, it is simply not possible for any ordinary Japanese person to identify a specific Malaysian dish' (Yoshino 2010).

Are consumers, such as tourists visiting Macau, able to name a Macau dish?[2] Tourists queue for pastéis de nata (egg tarts) at Lord Stow's in Coloane Village, for pork chop buns in the old Taipa village, and for almond cookies in various downtown locations. But the former is Portuguese (and in this case the 'secret' recipe is one created by an English chemist working in Macau, Andrew Stow (sadly deceased), who was playfully addressed as Lord Stow by the Portuguese community); and the latter two should technically be defined as 'Macau' food, the pork chop bun with Portuguese influence and the cookie with perhaps overseas Chinese influence combined with European.

Meanwhile, some elements of the Macan tourist crowd might be able to name African Chicken, and indeed this is sometimes referred to as the national dish of Macau. But could they, or would they, place this dish within the Macanese canon; and indeed would they even know of the existence of distinct Macanese foodways? Is pastéis de bacalhau (deep-fried cod-fish and potato croquettes) Portuguese, or Macanese, or both?

> 'There are many restaurants in Macau offering Portuguese and Macanese dishes but they are not explained properly so people do not know the difference.' —Graça Pacheco Jorge (personal correspondence, November 2017)

Now we explore the idea that diners do not know how to distinguish between Portuguese and Macanese dishes—and of course some Macanese dishes could be deemed to be originally Portuguese. In this case, then, Macanese dishes risk becoming 'lost' on a Portuguese menu. It was a cause for concern on the part of a number of respondents, represented here by the following two comments:

> 'Macanese cuisine is misunderstood in the sense that everything sold is considered Macanese when most dishes are of Portuguese origin. An effort should be made to clearly identify these in restaurant menus as a local authentic delicacy. Culinary heritage treasures. The cuisine is undoubtedly accepted as part of the culture but not disseminated accurately or effectively.' —Luis Lobo, assistant vice-president, Galaxy Entertainment Group (personal communication, November 2017)

'It [Macanese cuisine] is confused as being Portuguese in several restaurants. And the best is still cooked at home.' —Survey respondent

Historically, at least from the 1990s, many Hong Kongers would make the trek to Macau simply to order a plate of African Chicken (known in Portuguese as Galinha a Cafreal, literally 'blackened chicken'), a grilled dish prepared with chilli and coconut milk, among a few other ingredients. For many foodie tourists, Macau *was* or *is* African Chicken—and they would probably have considered it either as a Portuguese dish or as a Macau (as opposed to Macanese) dish alongside those pork chop buns and almond cookies. Very few would have had any idea that it was a Macanese dish, or even that separate Macanese foodways existed. On the other hand, many believe that the dish originated in Africa and thus claims that it is Macanese are inaccurate; and Goans might claim it as their own too. 'Galinha Africana is probably based on Galinha Cafreal from Mozambique, though some say it came to Macau via Goa' (Jorge da Silva 2016, 124). Indeed, the dish is referenced in a research paper on Goa, thus: 'Chicken Cafreal ... is originally from the Portuguese colonies in the African continent' (Nadkarni 2017, 321).

The cross-identity and geographical symbolism of African Chicken, 'created' in Macau in the 1940s, render it somewhat parallel to Singapore's iconic Fish Head Curry, which was surprisingly only introduced as recently as the early 1960s. This curry is commonly believed to be Indian: the spices used, and the cooking method, are almost identical to those for South Indian fish curry—but it was invented by a Malaysian chef. Yet South Asian cooking does not traditionally utilise the head of the fish. 'The dish itself is said to have been created to cater to Chinese tastes for the exotic ... it is now consumed by Indians as well as non-Indians' (Chua and Raja 2001, 185–86). Such dishes re-raise the question of hybridity versus creolisation.

In the view of Rufino Cabral, Macanese dishes are 'invisible' in Macau because of their 'affinity' with Chinese recipes. 'Many dishes considered Macanese, like peixe "cuscus", and cabbage with pork, etc, stem from Cantonese cuisine. There is only a slight difference in the preparation/finishing of the dishes, but they would not be seen as a major difference that can make them saleable as Macanese food, or be included in a menu in any Macanese restaurant' (personal communication, November 2017).

'Most of the authentic flavours are now replaced with more of suiting the Chinese palates from the visitors from Mainland.' —Susana Tsai (personal correspondence, November 2017)

A popular, scenic Portuguese restaurant that a decade ago was a key dining destination for the resident Portuguese community (including the then Portuguese Consul-General) has, over the years, gradually replaced square and rectangular tables suited for two or four guests respectively with round tables designed for groups of ten. This particular table format caters to the social dining habits of the local (Chinese) community that now frequents this place. Commentators say that this community has embraced this particular restaurant because there is ample parking; others say it is because local Chinese do not want to dine in the same places as (mainland) Chinese. In an attempt to cater to this newer clientele on the menu, the lines have been blurred between Macau's cuisines. For example, what is listed as a vegetable side dish of turnip tops (a very popular ingredient in Portuguese cooking) is in fact a plate of gai lan: one of the most popular green leafy vegetables in Cantonese cooking.

> 'Like all typical Portuguese restaurants outside Portugal, they adapt to customer and available product. Macau is not an exception. Some restaurants do a better job than others in what we would call authentic but some have developed a fusion of Portuguese and Macanese that satisfies the local community.' —Fausto Airoldi, production executive chef, food & beverage, culinary, Galaxy Macau (personal correspondence, September 2017)

It may be further mentioned that as the Macanese have increasingly married into the Chinese community rather than into the Portuguese community, particularly since the 1970s when this community started to shrink, cultural preferences themselves have become Cantonese ahead of Portuguese. This process has in turn affected the cuisine. Macanese cooking is something, according to one view, which owing to cultural change over time has 'progressed from traditional Portuguese cooking to something in between Portuguese and Asian/Chinese (traditional or original Macanese); to a cuisine that is today almost entirely Chinese-influenced (contemporary or new Macanese)' (Mamak 2007, 161). If the roots of Macanese food are agreed to be in the Portuguese tradition, it could be argued that the canon of recipes within Macau has become more 'local' as time has gone on, taking advantage of what is readily available and affordable in local markets. Chinese sausage (lap cheong) is sold at the market while Portuguese chouriço can really only be found in specialist shops or the odd supermarket. Bacalhau (salted codfish), once almost a daily staple, is now too expensive for regular home consumption.

Macanese Food as a Restaurant Food

> 'There are few restaurateurs who know Macanese food and many 'experts' who do not want to engage in the business.' —Rufino Cabral (personal correspondence, November 2017)

There has long been debate as to whether the Macanese cuisine, as one born in the domestic kitchen, constitutes a restaurant food—and most particularly in today's Instagram environment where taking a photograph of a beautifully presented dish is the new pre-eating ritual that has obliterated the saying of grace, or perhaps even the clinking of wine glasses over 'Cheers' or 'Bon appétit'.

> 'Our food takes a long time to produce. It is not so easy to commercialise. We have always eaten the real Macanese cuisine at family parties, in the family house, and at homes of other Macanese.' —Jorge Marreiros (personal conversation, May 2018)

As a cuisine born in the domestic kitchen, neither pretty plates nor profound presentation have ever been part of the cooking ethos.

> 'Many of the Macanese dishes are home cooked food, having not great aesthetic while presented as they are cooked and displayed as a table dish in a high-class restaurant (it would be good if someone could set up presentable Macanese dishes for a hotel restaurant!). Therefore, price of these dishes cannot be set at high, and the margin of profit is then small.' —Rufino Cabral (personal correspondence, November 2017)

There are no prominent Macanese chefs in Macau, or even enough professionally trained Macanese chefs, says Hugo Bandeira, food & beverage manager and lecturer at the Institute of Tourism Studies in Macau, an idea echoed by Rufino Cabral.

For Bandeira, this is part of the reason for the culinary 'confusion' around what constitutes Macanese foodways. Macanese food is widely described even in the professional culinary community as being a hybrid cooking, a mix of Portuguese and Chinese, but this is clearly incorrect. Bandeira also highlights the sometimes rather old-fashioned modes of preparation in the Macanese kitchen (the practice of cooking meat in its own blood, for example); unfashionable ingredients (lard would be a good example here); and the non-commercial nature of some of the highly time-consuming recipes, requiring a long list of ingredients, which can only be prepared in large quantities (such as Tacho).

For Portuguese hotel consultant Luis Heredia, an industry veteran in Macau, the solution is quite simple: modernity. It is often said that the Portuguese food in Macau is too basic and simple, but that is no longer the case, with ambitious young Portuguese chefs now eagerly cooking there and becoming part of the international movement for the transformation of Portuguese cuisine. 'We need chefs in Macau to say: What can we do with Macanese cuisine? And then run with it,' says Heredia. Right now, a prominent Portuguese chef such as Nuno Mendes has gained a loyal following for his Portuguese food in London, and the prominent Portugal-based chef José Avillez attracts foodie tourists to his restaurants and cafés in Lisboa and Porto. Yet at a contemporary, quality level, Macanese has virtually zero visibility outside Macau, and the situation is not much better in Macau. Heredia would like dynamic Portuguese chefs to change that.

The patrons of Portuguese and Macanese restaurants in Macau are principally divided among locals, visitors from Hong Kong, and a handful of international tourists. Yet the vast majority of tourists to Macau are mainland Chinese and, even if they want to take time to eat (the typical casino visitor takes a seven-minute break from gambling to consume a bowl of noodles, according to a researcher who was observing how the competition was faring when his own hotel was considering opening a new noodle bar), are most likely to eat in aspirational Michelin-starred Cantonese restaurants.

Government Initiatives: To Keep Macau's Culinary History Visible in Contemporary Landscapes?

'Because the cuisine is vanishing due to outward migration over decades, every effort in sharing recipes to perpetuate our identity as Macanese people is to be applauded. And the government should do more and more in this direction, subsidizing all business activity that strives to keep our heritage alive through this medium.' —Luis Lobo, assistant vice-president, Galaxy Entertainment Group (personal communication, November 2017)

'It [Macanese food] should be more present in the big restaurants in the main hotels.' —Survey respondent

In the broader context of a city becoming increasingly international in its culinary offerings, and boasting an impressive number of Michelin stars, a government regime is in place to encourage the promotion and sustainability of Portuguese and Macanese cuisines and Portuguese wine. Under this regime, five-star deluxe casino hotels are required by law to have three different types of restaurants, one of which must be Portuguese or Macanese. Under a separate regulation, all establishments—both new and existing—can apply for tax exemptions as a 'Tourism Utility' if they fulfil certain criteria. These include having on their menu 40 per cent of either Portuguese and/or Macanese traditional cuisine and 15 per cent Portuguese wine on wine lists.[3]

Co-founder of Riquexo café, Sonia Palmer, who also co-owns the outdoor-terraced Portuguese restaurant Miramar in Coloane, takes the view that, in reality, Macanese culinary initiatives often amount to little more than the occasional hotel promotion (personal correspondence, October 2017). Enforcing such provision would certainly be very difficult, and here we're back to the problem of definition.

Figure 2.2: Riquexo café, Macau. Photo courtesy of Sonia Palmer.

Independent restaurants that claim to be Macanese might be Portuguese; and a restaurant that claims to be Portuguese might be a Cantonese restaurant with chefs delivering their own take on Macanese food.

'It's wonderful that the government is doing their part to make sure we [Macau] don't lose the edge over other destinations, and protect its Portuguese culture, cuisine and heritage,' says Rutger Verschuren, general manager of Grand Lapa hotel (personal correspondence, October 2017). Perry Yuen, director of food and beverage at City of Dreams, concurs that such initiatives are good, 'but we need more quality people to lead the game,' he concludes (personal correspondence, October 2017). This situation might be helped by the announcement in the fourth quarter of 2017 that Macau had become a UNESCO Creative City of Gastronomy. But what happens once local foodways are 'sold' as part of the tourism package? What is being sold, and to whom?

Antonio Jorge da Silva wrote in 2016 about the inevitability, with Macau now being part of China, of Macanese cuisine becoming a restaurant commodity rather than something home-cooked: 'As the culture melds into that of the majority, so the cuisine will eventually become part of its historical past' (Jorge da Silva 2016, 61). It is widely argued that cultures, or cultural traits, disappear when they are no longer useful. In being part of a historical past, Macanese food, alongside all Portuguese cultural patterns, both tangible and intangible, could be seen to be useful: as part of a unique tourism offering. Yet what sort of transformative processes emerge when cuisines come under the tourist gaze?

What Does the Macau Tourist Think?

When, in a 2015 survey in Macau, tourists were asked to say the first word that came to mind in thinking about Macau, 'Casino/gambling' easily scored the highest with ninety-two hits—as against eleven hits for the word 'Cuisine'. But when they were given, to tick, a list of cultural elements such as Portuguese churches, Catholic religion, and variety of food, which they perceived as important for the image of Macau, 'Macanese cuisine' scored highly, second only to Portuguese architecture (Kong et al. 2015). However, it is unclear whether we are here specifically referring to Macanese cuisine or Macau's culinary offering in general, in which Cantonese cooking clearly dominates. There is a cultural anomaly here around the term 'Macanese', whereby it is often taken to mean anyone or anything from Macau.

Whichever culinary interpretation, it is clear that food is perceived as a significant part of Macau's 'unique' appeal, and while Hong Kong visitors (who make up 20.4 per cent of visitors) showed a particular predilection for the cuisine element of a visit, mainland Chinese (who make up 67.4 per cent of visitors) also expressed interest, which was perhaps a surprise finding given the stereotyped view of the mainland visitor who has zero interest in 'culture' but is only there for gambling.

Yang Zhang and Michael Hitchcock explored this notion in a genderised direction, noting that a significant percentage of female Individual Visitor Scheme tourists (as opposed to group travel) were not visiting Macau for gambling, but potentially for the more universally 'female' tourist interests of shopping, healthcare and eating out. Their methodology was 'web ethnography or netnography'. They write: 'Given the centrality of food and dining in Chinese culture, it is perhaps not surprising that restaurants, especially Portuguese ones, featured predominantly in the blogs of Chinese female tourists' (Zhang and Hitchcock 2014). Enthusiastic notes are recorded such as this from 'Sunny Flower': 'and had a great dinner in a fantastic Portuguese restaurant with my girlfriends'.

One restaurant is singled out as being particularly popular, translated into English as The Sailing, presumably referring to A Lorcha (the lorcha is a hybrid Portuguese-Chinese sailing boat designed in Macau), one of Macau's longest-standing and consistently good Portuguese-Macanese restaurants, which dates from the 1980s and was one of the first quality, independent restaurants of its kind. The account of 'Sunny Forest' indicates that the eating experience, while founded on fixed assumptions about European cooking, was a satisfying, explorative process. She ordered Portuguese Chicken (in fact a Macanese dish) and found it strange that it was not based on what to her were essential European ingredients—butter and tomato paste—and also that it was served with steamed rice, which she clearly did not consider to be European. The coconut cream and curry flavours made her believe she was eating a South East Asian dish. 'Anyway, white rice mixed with the curry sauce of Portuguese chicken tastes quite well matched and I learn about the Portuguese colonists' history of navigation through this dish since they brought different cooking ways and ingredients from different places that they came by and then created a new style' (Zhang and Hitchcock 2014). 'Sunny Forest' appears to have done some research into Macanese cuisine, aided perhaps by media: 'Chinese travel magazines present a multifaceted destination image to their readers with Macau focusing on history and heritage, places and attractions' (Kong et al. 2015).

Problems with Culinary Definitions in the Public Arena

There is much evidence of culinary confusion even within Macau's hospitality industry regarding Macanese cuisine. For example, the following are Portuguese and Macanese dishes listed on hotel restaurant menus. The Grand Lapa's Café Bela Vista menu includes no fewer than twelve Portuguese and Macanese dishes, such as Arroz de Pato (Duck Rice) and Galinha Piri Piri, which is translated into English on the menu as African Chicken. At Café Encore in Wynn Macau, the predominantly Chinese cuisine menu features a local page presenting Portuguese and Macanese dishes, including Fried Macanese Prawns, Bacalhau a Bras, and Caldo Verde. In Galaxy Macau's Gosto restaurant, specials might include Crab Curry and Baked Portuguese Chicken (in a saffron and coconut milk sauce).

Taking the dishes served in Grand Lapa, Galaxy, and Wynn, as listed above, Baked Portuguese Chicken is in fact a Macanese creation, known locally as Po Kok Kai (da

Silva 2016, 58–59). Galinha Piri Piri and African Chicken are actually quite separate dishes, the former likely to be of West African origin, while African Chicken is probably derived from a dish in Mozambique on the east coast of Africa (da Silva 2016, 124). Only Crab Curry and Fried Macanese Prawns could likely be considered 'authentically' Macanese, while Duck Rice, Bacalhau a Bras and Caldo Verde would be considered 'authentic' Portuguese—though this potato and cabbage soup is almost certainly made with the 'wrong' kind of cabbage in Macau.

While defining what's what proves to be problematic at the five-star hotel level, so it is even among the Macanese themselves. Two of the Macanese I dined with during my time in Macau in October 2017 separately declared that they 'had' to order Bacalhau whenever they were in a Portuguese/Macanese restaurant, thereby illustrating the importance placed on this Portuguese daily fare in the diet of the Macanese. One survey respondent declared the aforementioned Portuguese potato and cabbage soup, Caldo Verde, to be his favourite Macanese dish.

Such a culinary conversation goes in a number of directions. The Macanese cookbook *Taste of Macau: Portuguese Cuisine on the China Coast* contains a recipe for Bean Curd with Mushrooms (Jackson 2003, 92). Should a dish so decidedly Cantonese be included in a Macanese cookbook? Macau resident Edith Jorge, who offered the recipe, explained that it was a typical dish they would eat at home, and to which they might add leftovers such as tomato and lettuce. The Cantonese would be extremely unlikely to add such raw ingredients to this dish—so does that fact render this a Cantonese dish with a Macanese twist? It should also be noted that the Portuguese recipe canon—and thus the Macanese recipe canon—is not rich in vegetable dishes. The Portuguese traditionally consume vegetables and herbs (and legumes) daily but often as quite substantial soups, usually taken at the beginning of a meal, rather than as side dishes. (Historically, the thick soup, with perhaps a little chouriço added for meat protein, would have been the *only* dish at a meal.) The Macanese don't consume soup as enthusiastically as the Portuguese (and the Cantonese), so it could be deemed logical that they would borrow vegetable-based dishes from the Cantonese canon, according to what was seasonally available in the market, to sit alongside their own meat and fish dishes.

The Portuguese influence in Macau is unique, because nowhere else besides Macau within the Portuguese empire has a truly creolised foodway emerged. By comparison, the distinctive cooking of the Portuguese community in Malacca, the Kristang, was developed against the backdrop of existing Malay and Peranakan cuisines. Macanese cooking thus takes an important seat in the history of gastronomy. Together with Portuguese food and wine, it has become a visible part of the tourism package in Macau. But questions remain. How important a part? How visible is it?

A Culinary Hijacking?

Macanese food traditions may be perceived as today having a greater presence in Macau than ever before, but some Macanese say this comes not without a price. Macanese are fearful of losing their authentic cuisine, hijacked and de-authenticated not only by five-star hotels, but by local Cantonese restaurants, many of which—seizing a good business opportunity with traditional Cantonese fervour—now have a Macanese specialities page within their menu. The listed dishes, however, show significant Chinese interpretation. The ground pork and ground beef-based Minchi, as an example, might be served 'wet' rather than 'dry' and see the introduction of frozen green peas and small cubes of carrot. The claim has been made that (Chinese) chefs, who want to learn Macanese (and Portuguese) cooking, are not properly educated as to what constitutes Macanese cooking; or even if they are, they return to a (Chinese) kitchen and reinvent Macanese food—as opposed to modernising it, which would be more likely to be seen as acceptable.

Rather than being regarded as a historically important mutation of Portuguese cooking, and as a uniquely authentic cuisine rather than a creole cooking, the sense for Macanese cooking now is that it is now being reconfigured as a country cousin of Cantonese cooking. The cuisine is in danger of being subsumed, in exactly the same way that the broad brushstrokes of Macanese culture are disappearing as young Macanese become more and more assimilated into Chinese society.

This picks up the theme of the impossibility, at least from a Chinese perspective, of there being a non-Chinese culture, let alone an indigenous culture, in Macau. There is less and less incidence, or chance, of Macanese marrying into the Macanese culture and so, when Macanese food begins to be cooked by Chinese rather than Macanese (or even Portuguese), it begins the transformative process of becoming an aberration of local food culture. It becomes little more than Hong Kong's tea-coffee with condensed milk: a quaint nod in the direction of colonial cultural practices, but ultimately a denial.

> 'Macanese cuisine "subsumed"? I would like to think not . . . but that is [what is] happening. The [Macau] government gives us a nice little "pat [on the back]"—but at the end of the day we are all just Chinese . . . they don't understand that Beijing wants Macau to be different.' —Henrique Morais (personal conversation, Macau, October 2017)

One respondent believes that Minchi, given its near universal appeal, should be featured on coffee shop menus of five-star hotels in Asia, alongside such Asian culinary icons as Thai Green Chicken Curry, Indonesian Nasi Goreng, Malaysian Laksa, and Japanese Ramen noodles. Inclusion on such menus would be a rightful honour for Minchi, for sure; but it may just be that in such a representation Minchi becomes the lone symbol, the last memory, of Macanese cooking traditions.

Minchi: The Importance of Place

Here, we have examined the situation and status of Macanese food within Macau, with considerations regarding its resurgence versus its disappearance. What showed up very clearly in the research for this book was that Macanese in the diaspora hold a very special Macau in their hearts, and that may be an imagined Macau symbolised by a single dish—Minchi.

Is it possible that the recipe for a dish as part of a cuisine, or indeed the entire canon of recipes of which it is comprised, are so grounded in a place that they cannot be separated from it? In food studies, the notion of what constitutes a cuisine is an important theme. Distinctions are made between hybridisation (where culinary traditions and eating habits change within a culture) and creolisation (the combining of traditions and habits traditions from multiple culture for the creation of a new cuisine). Attempts at defining what a cuisine is are postulated; and the definition from perhaps the leading food anthropologist, Sidney Mintz, highlights how a sense of place is critical. This importance is clearly illustrated in this research on Macanese foodways. Here, from Mintz:

> Cuisines, when seen from the perspective of the people who care about the foods, are never foods of a country, but the foods of a place . . . I think a cuisine requires a population that eats that cuisine with sufficient frequency to consider themselves experts on it. They all believe, and care that they believe, that they know what it consists of, how it is made, and how it should taste. In short, a genuine cuisine has common social roots; is the food of a community. (Mintz 1996, 95–96)

> *Oh! A real pity, our Macau!*
> *What pain the heart will feel to see you have to go*
> *To leave our lives,*
> *To live separated from our Portugal.*[4]

A number of informants stressed the importance of the physical place called Macau and how their (loving) relationship with Macau can be seen as an important part of their cultural identity. Two respondents were very specific in the way that the dish Minchi is not just a dish. In some way it becomes the embodiment of Macau.

> 'Minchi is more than just a dish, it's a dish that in some way represents the Macanese as a whole and a comfort food. The mere mention of the word Minchi would indicate one's connection with Macau.' —Carlos Gutierrez (personal correspondence, November 2017)

The following statement illustrates how the notion of Minchi is immediately suggestive of a childhood in Macau; and the reference to the dish moves the writer seamlessly to the physical place of Macau:

> 'I like Minche [*sic*] and many others since childhood ages and when in Macau you are walking along the streets you feel like that you belong there and since the long

absence you feel like you were born again there. I believe that any other Macaense born will have the same feeling as myself about Macau.' —André Amante (personal correspondence, November 2017)

Macau has physically changed so much from the days when a single bridge linked the peninsula with the island of Taipa, itself connected to Coloane with a causeway laid by the Portuguese military before they left. Macau is now effectively a solid landmass rather than a peninsula and two islands. And, of course, it has changed so much beyond what can be seen physically. Yet there is a strong sense that it is *still Macau*; it has been transformed in the minds of many Macanese into an *imagined* Macau. With the loss of Macau, with its 'return' to the motherland, the Macanese have, politically at least, lost their physical 'place'; but Macau has assumed another form in memory.

'As a Macanese, I feel our food is an important link back to Macau, as well as all the way back to Portugal. But I fear the loss of this linkage as Macau's current prominence rises globally.' —Ed Rozario (personal correspondence, 2012)

The importance of place itself is an important finding of Jean Duruz's research, drawing on Wendy Hutton's arguments in *The Food of Love: Four Centuries of East-West Cuisine*.[5] Duruz explores what she hesitatingly calls 'Eurasian' cuisines, in particular those of Colombo, Malacca, Penang, and Singapore, and reaches the following conclusion: 'I am speculating that, under particular historic conditions of "openness" (as in port cities of the Indian Ocean and the Strait of Malacca), and within relations that allow exchanges (for example, in communities drawing on Christian beliefs, where food taboos are less in evidence), the "place" itself represents important contributing capital to sustain economies of love and the "food of love" itself' (Duruz 2016). The parallels with Macanese foodways within the context of port cities are evident; and indeed the implicit culinary conversations emanating between these various communities have begun to be explored elsewhere in this book (see Chapters 4 and 5).

History of Portuguese/Macanese restaurants in Macau

Long before the huge solid, golden block that is SANDS, or the jagged, towering edges of the Grand Lisboa were defining the skyline—so let's go back two decades, and even as far as the 1970s—it was the back streets that were the destination: a culinary destination. Until the 1980s, there were almost no Portuguese restaurants in Macau. In fact, there were probably few 'restaurants' at all; rather casual street dining venues and cafés. Only one or two of the better hotels would have had (Western) restaurants. Portuguese expatriates have traditionally cooked Portuguese for themselves at home or eaten at one or two downtown locations, such as Solmar or the (formerly members-only but now open to the public) dining room of Clube Militar.

Portuguese wine was already visible, however. Hong Kong restaurateur (the owner of Kin's Kitchen) and cultural commentator Lau Kin Wai explains that Mateus Rosé was the first grape wine to which many Hong Kongers would have been introduced. On visits in the 1970s to then Portuguese-administered Macau (a journey that would have taken more than three hours on the slow ferry), they could drink a bottle of this slightly sweet, slightly fizzy rosé in a dai pai dong (a café selling local Cantonese food) such as dominated the dining scene in this period (though there were a few expensive Cantonese restaurants on Rua da Felicidade serving (now controversial) delicacies such as shark's fin and bird's nest) and bring a bottle home to Hong Kong too. In this period of Macau's (not so good) economic fortunes, the idea of French wine was simply too expensive to entertain.

By the 1980s, the population of Macau had swollen by half, to around 400,000, the majority of new arrivals coming from across the border with China (Gongbei-Zhuhai), but these immigrants were largely workers, as opposed to the kind of big-shot entrepreneurs who would frequent expensive restaurants, though many would open their own small businesses.

There was little fine (French or European) dining at this time and into the 1980s in Macau. There was little cultural demand for it and little leisure money to pay for it, for Macau would have to wait until 2002 (the year of the opening of the colossal SANDS casino near the Ferry terminal, after the deregulation of casino licences) to feel again like the Venice—and this time also like the Las Vegas—of the East. A Galera in Hotel Lisboa held the fort for more expensive Portuguese/Western dining, and Italian food had started to go a touch upmarket, first with Mezzaluna in the Mandarin Oriental; but the most prestigious European restaurant to open in Macau was Robuchon a Galera (2001), not only supplanting the Portuguese restaurant A Galera but also supplanting or suppressing any notion of status for Portuguese food in Macau. Later, though, Hotel Lisboa was to open Guincho a Galera (2011) after Portuguese food back home in Portugal was starting to gain traction, as a kind of branch of the Michelin-starred Fortaleza do Guincho—just up the beach from the fishing village of Cascais, just north of Lisboa.

By the early 1990s, a lively local Portuguese restaurant scene was emerging, and Macau became an inexpensive and slightly exotic culinary destination. Hong Kongers would take the (one hour fast) ferry over for Sunday lunch, quite possibly to Fernando's (Fernando, incidentally, was born in the Azores) on Coloane island's Hac Sa Beach. Casual but appealing and welcoming restaurants such as Petisquera, A Lorcha, and Coloane Village's Caçarola (now Espaço Lisboa) opened and gained good reputations but their easy, accessible, 'mom and pop' image prevailed over prestige and price. Two rather stylish Macanese restaurants were also coming into view. The first was the relatively mainstream Flamingo in the Hyatt Regency on Taipa, with the ever-friendly Chef Chan—who comes from a family of ethnically Cantonese chefs—in charge of the kitchen. The dining space was delightfully landscaped around an ornamental pond, home to a number of flamingos. The second was the more eclectic Balichão, which first opened on the ground floor of the popular apartment block Hoi Fu, with striking art on the walls. Isabel Eusebio ran front of house while her mother, Maria Eusebio, was in charge of the kitchen. Both restaurants are long gone. The former closed down when the Hyatt's management contract expired;[6] the latter moved to a lovely setting in Coloane Park, but business suffered in what was then viewed as a remote location. The same park today faces a busy residential area of apartment blocks.

The Portuguese have influenced cuisines across Asia and far beyond the Columbian Exchange, in the course of which newly introduced foodstuffs changed agriculture and diets as well as lives. This influence has shown itself most particularly in the pastry kitchen, where egg yolk and sugar rule, and also in the use of vinegar in cooking—see a discussion of Vindaloo in Chapter 4. Portuguese foodways have also influenced places, most particularly Macau, where Portuguese food remains more popular than French in the everyday sense. Even within the current decade more and more Portuguese restaurants have been appearing in the shiny, buzzing, and contemporary Macau, joining the ranks of those establishments that have for three decades been serving the old favourites—Caldo Verde (potato and cabbage (couve) soup), Bacalhau a Bras (salt cod with fried potato and onion), Açorda de Marisco (seafood cooked with bread), and the Alentejo dish of pork cooked with clams and bay leaf.

Among the newcomers, few are serving anything close to the 'contemporary' Portuguese food of top Portuguese chefs in Europe, Nuno Mendes in London and José Avillez at home in Lisboa and Porto, preferring to offer the 'old favourites', as mentioned above, which have proven to be so popular. While such restaurants are part of the eating fabric for locals of all nationalities, they form an important part of the tourism package, in which Macau is distinguished from other southern Chinese or regional cities not only because of its gambling offer, but because of its uniquely long European-influenced history.

'I only see this trend going from strength to strength,' says Luis Lobo, on the subject of Portuguese and Macanese culinary culture in Macau (personal correspondence, November 2017). As an assistant vice-president with Galaxy Entertainment Group who is in fact himself Macanese, Lobo is there on the front line. 'These days there is a flourish of new small authentic restaurants with owners coming from Portugal or ex-Portuguese colonies. These are welcome entries because authenticity in the age of foodies is a must-have for a tourist destination.' He asserts that there is a growing number of visitors arriving in Macau looking not for a casino experience, but for a cultural one.

Conclusion

Macanese food, if rooted in Portuguese cooking traditions, is sometimes confused with it. As the decades and even centuries have passed, those Portuguese origins have become more obscured, with the gradual substitution of local market ingredients over specialist imports: local pork meat sausage lap cheong over the use of Portuguese chouriço, for example. Other adaptations are occurring, often in relation to global dietary fads. Whether or not it is seen to be visible in Macau may depend on whether you believe it doesn't exist in restaurants but only in the home; whether you believe that it can be served in Cantonese restaurants, or indeed in Portuguese restaurants; or whether you believe it 'works' as restaurant food at all. Even the industry seems unsure of how it fits in the canon of local (Cantonese) dishes and 'local' (Portuguese) dishes, or even just 'Macau' dishes. Further confusion arises as it becomes part of the tourism package, transformed and reproduced to meet the expectations of the visitor—and in terms of how those expectations might be framed.

3
The Loss of a Cuisine and the Practice of Recipe Sharing

'Forgive me if I decide to be like my grandmother and grand-aunts and great-grandmother in being judicious about who I share what [recipes] with... hopefully someone will come along who I can personally transmit these to. That person will understand this and will need to have an intrinsic commitment to cooking.' —Macanese, resident in California, aged forty-three (personal correspondence, 2012)

'I think the saddest thing is that because of the older generation, not sharing recipes outside the family... slowly we are losing the real Macanese recipes.' —Isabela Costa (personal conversation, Macau, October 2017)

In Chapter 2 we worked towards an understanding of the extent to which Macanese food is visible in Macau. If it isn't particularly visible there, in its homeland, what other spaces might it inhabit? Might it exist in the memory or in the collective memory, for example, or perhaps today more often in the written recipe? Twenty-five years ago, some Macanese were already worried that their cuisine was disappearing, even within their own community, because in their view knowledge was not being sufficiently passed on in the oral tradition of the culture.

In this chapter I examine the practice of recipe sharing, a practice that has historically been controversial among the Macanese; though it is questioned as to whether such a propensity for discretion is unique to this ethnic community. Touched upon is the nature of the recipe itself, how it might be transmitted and recorded—from being part of an oral tradition, to being available in the relatively new recipe-sharing forum of the internet, through to being part of a cookbook published and distributed in the public and global domain.

Why ask a question about the sharing of recipes in the survey? Over time, many or most Macanese have been reluctant to share Macanese recipes, except within the family (though there are exceptions or nuances even there), or possibly within the broader Macanese community, but almost certainly not beyond it and into wider society. I had personal experience of this when in 2002 I began research for my Macanese cultural cookbook *Taste of Macau: Portuguese Cuisine on the China Coast*, which was published in 2003. Those who collaborated with me were singularly those who were already concerned about the threat of the disappearance of Macanese cuisine. The Macanese community in Hong Kong was particularly engaged with my work. On the other hand, one Macanese friend in Macau, who was very supportive of my research, asked her father for access to their family recipes. He refused, on the grounds that he suspected her of—passing them to me. There is a shared oral tradition of recipe transmission, which would occur within families and communities; but this is an example of the historical reluctance to share recipes outside a family or community.

What sort of shape might this reluctance to share take, and could this predilection be unique to the Macanese? I put a very specific statement, as above, in the survey, in the hope of gaining some insights. After all, because Macanese cooking was born in the domestic kitchen, could not recipes by definition be family recipes; family heirlooms? However, Macanese cooking was born in a myriad of domestic kitchens and then emerged as a 'new' foodway, defined as such through the culinary collusion of the broader community. Sharing was definitely happening, however informal that sharing was: chats between cooks and servants across garden walls, perhaps, and between wives out for a stroll, all of which could encourage the tweaking of ingredients and technique.

I also wanted to see if there might be a correlation between cultural identity and the sharing of recipes, and what shape that process could take and why. If Macanese food is an important part of cultural identity, might that lead to an enthusiasm for sharing recipes beyond the ethnic community? Recipe sharing could be seen as a sharing of the Self with the Other; an authentication of a culture largely invisible, even in Macau itself. A huge majority of people have never heard of Macau, let alone the foodways of the Macanese. Or is there a sense that because Macanese cooking is one of the last tenets of cultural identity within the community, recipes become a sacred possession not to be shared? They become family possessions, across generations, which should stay within the family.

What space is occupied by Macanese food, within Macau? Are there further considerations with regard to practices of sharing recipes within but perhaps not beyond the Macanese community that might be unique to the Macanese in the context of Macau? We might consider that in the case of Macanese cooking the situation is further nuanced by the status of Macanese food within Macau. It would be a very broadly accepted notion that the 'national' or 'indigenous' food of Macau is Cantonese (Chinese). Thus, the Macanese, who consider themselves the *filhos* (sons) of Macau, or 'born of the land' (de Pina-Cabral 2002, 71), retain a complicated, even uneasy relationship with a place that is now governed by Beijing; by the 'Chinese'. Any identity that pre-handover in 1999 might have centred on Portuguese-ness was to be challenged and pushed towards a Chinese alignment. (Macanese children applying to local schools have to assume a Chinese family name, for example.) Whether such moves reinforce Macanese-ness and thus render group identity ever stronger, or result in a dilution or repression of Macanese-ness, is an area that could be further researched in the arena of cultural anthropology.

Recipes in a Broader Context: A Theoretical Approach

It is an interesting debate, perhaps an aside, as to whether recipes should be covered by copyright. But to look at recipes in this context may deepen our understanding as to what (in their phases of being written, recorded, and distributed) recipes are, what they mean, and to whom. Courts have made distinction between what is fact (discovered but not created) and what is created (a new and distinct discovery). The example can be given of the status of a humble American apple pie versus Thomas Keller's 'Oysters & Pearls'—a dish elaborated with tapioca pudding, Malpeque oysters, and caviar.[1] Recipes are defined as representing functional directions for achieving a certain result, in this case something that resembles a community understanding of the nature of apple pie. The recipe relays a set of facts, such that for the making of apple pie one first requires apples, and then pastry, and that the two must then be baked together. By contrast, Keller did not read a recipe for and then reproduce 'Oysters & Pearls'. He created the dish (Buccafusco 2007). It might thereafter be surmised that should other chefs wish to reproduce this dish in their own restaurants, it would be listed on the menu as 'Chef Keller's Oysters & Pearls,' and might even mention the name of the restaurant where it was served for the first time. We might here ponder, in the Macanese context, whether African Chicken, when it was launched at the Pousada de Macau in the 1940s, could have been correctly, or alternatively, named Chef Angelo's Galinha a Cafreal.

I find it interesting to use the model outlined above—fact versus creation—as a way of approaching the sharing of recipes within the Macanese community. Clearly, we are not necessarily talking about copyright in the publishing sense, but we are talking about the process of introducing recipes into the public domain. I believe that what we can identify in Macanese recipes, recorded or otherwise, is a confluence of family and community. We are in agreement within the Macanese community that, say, Porco Bafassa is a Macanese dish, even if you use Chinese rice vinegar and sweet sherry in your pork marinade, while I use Portuguese white wine. Your Capela (pork meat loaf) might taste good enough, but I incorporate onion and garlic in mine.[2] By having and quite possibly guarding our own family's passed-down recipe, we are also positing the dual importance of individual families—and their own individual tastes and preferences—within the broader Macanese community in the construction of cultural identity. This, in particular, takes us back to the subject of mother, her mother, and mothers through generations before that.

What is notable, given the existence of a Macanese recipe Anthology from Shanghai, the sharing of recipes has a long history (from at least the 1930s)—but that history belongs in the realm of diaspora, rather than forming part of a being-Macanese-in-Macau trajectory. In order to reinforce the sense of cultural identity in the diaspora, community seems to enter a realm in which it overrides family. The sharing of recipes, the cooking of Macanese food, the eating of it, and the sharing of it are intertwined in a more complicated manner when we are beyond Macau. We might put it thus: I am Macanese because I cook and eat Macanese food at home, but I identify even more strongly as Macanese when I eat it with other members of the community beyond my own home. However, almost every recipe in the Anthology is credited to someone by name, allowing for the family/personal still to exist within the broader community.

Recipe sharing within the Macanese community, and within other communities

None of this is at all to say that issues around the exclusive sharing of recipes within families is unique to the Macanese, and I here mention at least one book and one study so as to help illustrate this point. Michael Lee West's *Consuming Passion* is a cookbook-cum-memoir that describes the author's childhood—and adulthood—in the Louisiana Delta and Tennessee. She emphasises competitive culinary activity among women with the attendant secrecy around recipes: 'She always promised to give me her recipe [for potato salad], but she'd get tongue-tied and leave out essential ingredients' (Lee West 1999, 87); and also addresses the paradox of formalising, through the written word, an oral culinary tradition.

In Melbourne, Australia, a study was undertaken of the kind of informal/home-made cookbooks that exist across borders and boundaries. Scrapbooks of recipes had been assembled from a multitude of sources, including handwritten, photocopied recipes inserted in plastic pockets, newspaper tear-outs smeared in butter, and typed recipes annotated with scribbles by the latest incumbent. Of particular note is a volume entitled *Nana's Recipes*, which has a picture of Nana on the front, illustrative of a tremendously personalised vision of recipe sharing and showing how even production of the volume remained tightly within the family. 'This cookbook was a record of the meals shared within the family. The grandchildren were asked individually, what their favourite Nana recipes were, and Nana then wrote these out by hand. A cousin then compiled all the recipes, photocopied them, bound and distributed a copy to each.' The researchers envisaged in conclusion 'the homemade family cookbook as a significant material and cultural artefact in the family kitchen' (Davis et al. 2014). This intra-family communication was a process far deeper than the simple act of Nana sharing recipes in her dotage.

Family scrapbooks in this built-up-over-time genre were mentioned during the Macanese survey. Respondents used phrases such as 'we have our own family recipes' and 'I have my own home recipes'. But more formalised organisations of recipes were also referred to. One respondent said their repertoire 'includes hand written family recipes shared by aunts, cousins, friends etc.'; another wrote: 'I use hand down family recipes generally from old scrap books and only occasionally from a Macanese cookbook'; and another indicated they did not have any formal documentation 'except one my mom copied when my great-grandmother cooked'.

Revealed by the Melbourne 'Nana' study is a dynamic forum in which the family recipients of such scrapbooks work with, but also play with, the recipes, whether as a consequence of dietary fads and fashions, personal preferences, time constraints, or simply a more cosmopolitan approach to cooking. 'And then when I've cooked it I make some variations and document the variations [in the cookbook]'; 'and so I'll combine two or three recipes into one': 'Like they're never hot enough, I always put more chili than they say'; 'Lemon slice is a really good one to do with the kids, but it is a bit of pain as you have to crush the biscuits with a rolling pin and a plastic bag' (Davis et al. 2014). Time consuming, indeed—at least in the eyes of the younger generation!

We see just these kinds of adaptations being enacted as Tony da Silva (sometimes) modifies his mother's (on occasion somewhat incomplete) Macanese recipes ready for his 2016 publication *Macaense Cuisine: Origins and Evolution*. He might 'delete' the Lea & Perrins of which she was so keen, segment a chicken rather than cooking it whole for Galinha Saffrang, use chicken stock instead or water for Galinha com Rabano, and create a much more sophisticated rendition of Porco Bafassa. For his mother's recipe for Christmas Cake, he asked his (English) wife, Penelope, to add in details of method—which his mother had assumed would/should have been known by any cook and had thus omitted (Jorge da Silva 2016).

A key difference between the family-kitchen examples explored by Hilary Davis at Melbourne, together with her co-authors, is that in the Macau context Macanese family recipes and scrapbooks have traditionally existed against a backdrop of an entire absence of widely available recipe reference books of their own cuisine.

A sense of family

> Family, to most of the Macanese I know, is still important and cherished. It warms my heart to see my children, Makena and Colin, loving my father, their cousins, aunts and uncles as deeply as we loved our four aunts. (Webster 2012)

Certainly, the results of this culinary research revealed a strong sense of family attachment and identity, in addition to a broader Macanese cultural identity within the Macanese community. How might this affect the sharing of recipes? For example, for one respondent the 'handing down' (implicit in this terminology is that the sharing takes place strictly within the family, and to the younger generation) of recipes and traditions lies at the heart of his sense of identity derived through Macanese food, in order that 'the culture will not be lost' (personal correspondence, November 2017).

The importance of family is even reflected in the titles of some Macanese cookbooks such as *A Cozinha de Macau de Casa Meu Avô* (translation: The kitchen of Macau from the house of my grandfather) by Graça Pacheco Jorge, and *Traditional Recipes from my Auntie Albertina* by Cintia Conçeicão Serro, published in Canada. Antonio M. Jorge da Silva's cookbook is generically entitled *Macaense Cuisine: Origins and Evolution*—but the cover shot is an image of his (very elegant) mother preparing an apparently rather elaborate dish; see below.

Informants have consistently stressed the importance of cooking their own family recipes.

Figure 3.1: Book cover. Photo courtesy of Cintia Conçeicão Serro.

Figure 3.2: Olga A. Pacheco Jorge da Silva. This image appears on the cover of Antonio M. Jorge da Silva's cookbook *Macaense Cuisine*. Photo courtesy of Olga A. Pacheco Jorge da Silva.

> 'Every family has a minchi [recipe]. Do you use "tik yau" or treacle or some other "secret ingredient"?[3] There are obvious slight differences, and every family treasures their own.' —Anthony Cabral (personal correspondence, November 2017)

> 'Cooking traditional dishes needs to be from the heart in order to be shared with those who are partaking in the meal and not just for the sake of cooking the dish according to recipes handed down for the sake of having a meal.' —Vitor Souza (personal correspondence, November 2017)

> 'Even if you share the recipes, there is still a personal touch that is hard to follow.' —Survey respondent

> 'I love home cooked Macanese meals prepared by my Mum.' —Survey respondent

Implicit is a connection with mother, with grandmother, with great-grandmother; and further back than that. The importance of the mother figure is implicit in the generalised Macanese adoption of Portuguese family name presentation, whereby the mother's maiden name is included in front of the father's family name—although it would seem that few Macanese actually utilise such cumbersome family names any longer. On the other hand, the notion of ancestor worship, while being far from central in Portuguese and generic European culture, is important for the Macanese. This practice would have historically been affirmed within Macau through the everyday acts of the local Cantonese population, for whom ancestor worship remains a critical cultural notion. To cook the dish of the ancestor is to respect that ancestor. Tony da Silva puts it this way:

> 'Food is a very strong tie to many cultures and its connection to the actual preservation of the culture is not as important as the memory of its taste and its relation to some ancestor or other who had prepared the dish.' (personal correspondence, 2012)

Family rivalry?

Might family rivalry emerge as a result of this existence of tight-knit generational structures, meaning that recipes were regarded as family secrets; that each family considered their rendition of, say, Capela, the best, the authentic, the ultimate dish?

> 'Of course in the past there was rivalry between the families, it was a question of showing who made the best meals, parties and receptions, with the finest and more genuine recipes.' —Graça Pacheco Jorge (personal correspondence, November 2017)[4]

> 'I don't think there is any real rivalry among families, it's just a way every family uses different ingredients to cook the same dish in their own unique way.' —Vitor Souza (personal correspondence, November 2017)

As described in Appendix 2, in the context of the cooking competitions held as part of the regular Encontro meetings of the Macanese diaspora in Macau, opinions are divided on the matter of family rivalry,[5] and the extent to which this might have contributed to an air of secrecy around recipes. This culture of secrecy has been placed in an historical context as shared by this Macanese respondent:

> 'I feel that most families don't like to share their recipes as they want to be considered the best. If their secrets are out, they would not carry on this position. You have to think that some time ago, the circle was very small and there were many good cooks around. The old ladies were very conscious of their 'bestness' in the small society and cooking was essential to identify families. A duck's egg or a touch of Chinese wine in a specific dish was basically the difference and they were happy to pass this secret to their immediate family, only, but not to anyone else. Many good secrets were then lost.' —Rufino Cabral (personal correspondence, November 2017)

To share or not to share?

'Cuisine belong with the performing arts, and as for other such arts, the social survival of the culinary performance depends on words.'[6] —Priscilla Parkhurst Fergusson

In the recipe Anthology, mentioned throughout this text, which was put together in Shanghai but was also circulating in Hong Kong and arrived in my own hands, a

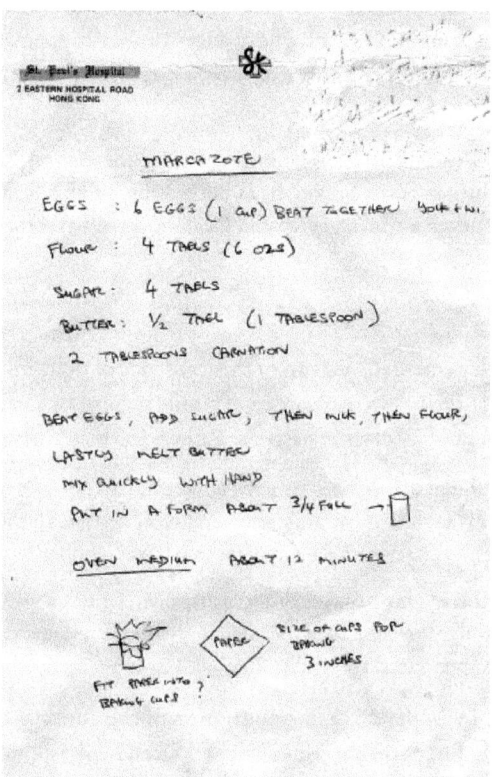

Figure 3.3: An annotation from the Anthology of Macanese recipes.

strong culture of sharing recipes is revealed—together with some gentle rivalry. The editor picks what s/he considers to be the best of the entries for, say, Porco Balichão Tamarinho. Another version is recorded, perhaps pejoratively, as being a 'modern', meaning time-saving, rendition of this recipe. The cuisine, then, was already being affected by contemporary lifestyle mores.

There are some other rather fascinating inclusions to consider in the particular context of sharing. We here return briefly to Michael Lee West's *Consuming Passions* in which she writes about the reluctance of her family and friends to pass on recipes, and she makes explicit the relationship between the transmission (of recipes), writing, and death. She recounts a conversation at a funeral, when an aunt lamented that her grandmother is said to have taken her gingerbread recipe to the grave, just as her mother before her took the one for her special biscuits. 'Food is a dying art . . . at least in this family. We're burying our best recipes' (Lee West 1999, 7). This idea of 'burying' recipes seems to be particularly pertinent in the Macanese context, the idea having been expressed that the 'best' recipes may already have gone to the grave (see, for example, Jorge 2004, 10); but the idea is coming through from this research that there's a swell of opinion to avoid that continuing to happen. Let's take an actual example.

Amidst the carefully typed-out recipes in the Macanese recipe Anthology, there's a handwritten note. This is a recipe for the sweet snack called Marcazote. The note includes little diagrams illustrating shapes and sizes, and shows how to fold these snacks correctly. Measures in taels are at one point converted into ounces, and later into tablespoons. Most strikingly, it is written on the letterhead of Hong Kong's St. Paul's Hospital on Eastern Hospital Road. This is an extraordinary document. Does the writing on hospital letterhead suggest a deliberate attempt to *not* take a recipe to the grave? Perhaps it was written by a mother or, more likely, given the conversion of taels to more standard contemporary weights and measures, by a daughter (or son), and merely dictated by the mother. It might raise a question about, in the event of writing one's will, whether one considers recipes as heirlooms to be passed on. Would this process even occur to a parent or grandparent?

Here are two examples of just such an omission before death.

'My Granny was famous for her sarrabulho [a dish redolent with spice, made from pig blood and chicken offal] and I was lucky enough to have tried it during my teenage years; but sadly she didn't leave the recipe written down for anyone. Those who remember say that when she cooked it, the whole neighbourhood would know, because of the unique aromas. I tried to reproduce it, and am glad to say I succeeded, but it took me almost five hours in the kitchen to achieve the correct aroma and taste.'
—Marina de Senna Fernandes (Jackson 2003, 28)

'Sadly, many of the recipes in the Macanese repertoire we only know by name and have no idea how to actually make them. My nickname is Mutchi, after a Macanese sweet dumpling called muchi-muchi . . . I have learnt that there is only one person in Macau who really knows how to make it.' —Marina de Senna Fernandes (Jackson 2003, 28)

On the other hand, we have examples of women who deliberately kept recipes secret, even within the confines of the family.

> 'Being a typical older-generation Macanese, she [the maternal grandmother] did not believe in passing on her knowledge of the world's greatest cuisine and everyone, including myself, was shooed out of the kitchen!' —Anabela Estorninho (Jackson 2003, 24–25)

Here it can be argued that knowledge can be seen as being equal to power, thus recipes were not even transmitted within the family. The (grand)mother not only 'owned' her own recipe but wanted to be seen (and remembered?) as someone akin to 'the family's sole source of perfect food. Mama doesn't like rivals in the kitchen' (Lee West 1999, 83).

There is a tension between the sense of love and family as embodied in a dish, and the idea of commodifying that dish through writing down the recipe. Have we lost something here, such as authenticity; or gained something, such as a written social history? Or both? This struggle between modernisation and traditional ways of transmitting family tradition is also suggestive of the fact that children or young people don't any longer aspire to become a replica of their own mother and cook as she cooks, and thus don't want to spend time in the kitchen, as their mother did with her own mother (see, for example, Sutton 2001, 169).

The subject of transmission of culinary knowledge is further nuanced in the Macanese cuisine because of the diaspora and the subsequent intermarrying with other cultures. What space does the recipe, whether existing in memory or in a cookbook, now inhabit, and how would or should it be shared? Perhaps such questions, and their potential answers, help us to understand the ambivalence with which cookbooks are viewed within the Macanese community, as explored later in this chapter.

Contemporary attitudes to sharing recipes

Certainly, in the course of this research project, the question of the sharing of Macanese recipes evoked some strong emotion. Respondents used words such as 'selfishness' and 'stupidity', or 'disappointed', to describe their attitude to those who have refused to share. 'Recipes should be for anyone. Free,' asserted one respondent.

> 'Old ladies saw themselves as guardians of something almost sacred. One hundred years ago it was OK not to share recipes. During or since the last fifty years, it is just selfish.' —Jorge Marreiros (personal conversation, May 2018)

> 'I always give my recipes to people who ask me, I feel this way the Macanese food will not die and will have the genuine ingredients.' —Sonia Palmer, owner, Riquexo café (personal correspondence, December 2017)

Some responded to the sharing question with additional comments such as 'I share with my son' or 'among younger Macanese family members', indicating that secrecy at least within families remains normalised in some quarters. A handful of respondents said that they simply didn't have any recipes; and one respondent was unsure what was meant by sharing recipes. Did cooking for someone else count as sharing, or did I mean literally giving them a handwritten recipe?

João de Pina-Cabral asserts that when the Macanese were forced to harness their Portuguese cultural capital over their uniqueness, it came at a cost: the gradual disintegration of their Creole. 'Their language (the *patuá*) first became a domestic female language and then vanished totally in favour of Portuguese or English; their special manner of dressing was abandoned; and they started practising forms of marriage and of selective genealogical memory that emphasized Europeanness' (de Pina-Cabral 2002, 67). There are two particular points of interest here. First is that the patuá, which comprises similar cultural juxtapositions as the cooking, was, just like the cuisine, of domestic origin. The second point of interest is that food is not mentioned here. How is it that the cooking seems to have survived? It might be construed that it is the very domestic nature of it—it is something consumed privately at home, unlike a patuá or a mode of dressing, which form part of the public arena.

A few Macanese, most particularly in Macau, have tried to preserve the patuá—though literally in theatrical performance rather than in a quotidian sense—but it can directly be observed that Macanese food is perhaps the remaining, and thus highly significant, indicator of cultural identity. This being the case, perhaps you want to keep your recipes and your deep understanding of the cuisine, as they're all that is left of your Macanese-ness? If there are indeed family reasons, in addition to broader historical cultural ones, for not sharing recipes, what of the feeling today? Today, the loss would surely be not a cultural one of face among families, or of community status; but the almost literal loss of a 450-year-old culinary culture.

> 'I'm not one of those women who feel their cookies are their "grandmother's secret". That's what an Austrian woman told me once. How stupid can you get? If Macanese families are like that, I'm not impressed. Part of their identity—*and that is why they don't want to share*?' —Patricia da Silva (personal correspondence, November 2017) (my emphasis)

Indeed, Macanese food takes on importance at many levels beyond the spoon and fork. Man shall not live by bread alone. Macanese food goes far beyond calories, nutrients, and sustenance.

> 'I do my best to cook for my grandchildren at every opportunity *so that the tastes will be embedded in them* from a young age.' —Henri de Souza (personal correspondence, November 2017) (my emphasis)

> 'Most of us of the Macanese diaspora cling to our heritage, like most migrants, via our traditional food.' —Bosco Correa (personal correspondence, 2012)

So it can be argued that the relationship of the Macanese to Macanese food is profoundly complex; and further, occupies multiple spaces—in the domestic setting, in Macau the place, and within the global diaspora. 'Food provides a fluid symbolic medium for making statements about identity' (James 1997, 74). For Macanese in the diaspora, the question arises as to the nature of their relationship with the food of their host country, though not many included comments about what other kinds of food they might eat beyond Macanese; some mentioned Chinese and Japanese; and perhaps a daughter-in-law who liked to cook Italian. A Macanese living in Portugal mentioned that they also like Portuguese food. Marina Emam, who lives in Australia and is married to an Egyptian, wrote that she had added Middle Eastern cuisine to her home life; and that Portuguese and Chinese cooking were also still part of her repertoire (personal correspondence, November 2017).

Only a single informant out of the total of 241 claimed to never eat Macanese food; less than 1 per cent said they strongly disagreed that it was their favourite cuisine; and I personally have never met a Macanese who said they didn't like Macanese food: most drool over the mention of Minchi. Indeed, most are tremendously proud of their cuisine. More than 20 per cent of respondents strongly agreed that Macanese is their favourite cuisine—even if they only eat it annually. Many respondents clearly generously share their cuisine with non-Macanese friends and family—they cook for them, even if they don't actually share written recipes—and certainly the cuisine has a broad cross-cultural appeal. Who wouldn't like Minchi?!

Several respondents indicated that they do share actual recipes beyond the family or Macanese community. For example:

> 'I am happy to share recipes from whomever requests them as these dishes have proved very popular with our dinner guests. We also share recipes within our extended family.' —Antonia Lai (personal correspondence, November 2017)

> 'I would be very happy to share. That being said, I don't have many or those I know are from memory. For recipes I would have to defer to my sister.' —James Nobre (personal correspondence, November 2017)

Here, our respondent raises another interesting issue, which is that many Macanese don't or have never had recipes because they simply learned to cook by watching, and today cook from memory. Again, these losses of recipes are not necessarily as a result of a deliberate act. The role of memory in the reproduction of Macanese food is another important component here.

> 'Many from the community claim they have the "real" (authentic) recipe for one dish or another, forgetting that "real" is only their interpretation of the tastes they remember.' —Tony da Silva (personal correspondence, 2012)

> 'Sadly, with age the memory can play tricks on the taste buds. One example is the search for Angelo's African Chicken. Within our community around the world, there are legions of amateur cooks experimenting with various ingredients to replicate this famous dish. Funnily, with the passage of time, if we were presented today with a chicken cooked by Angelo himself, we might not recognise it.' —Ed Rozario (personal correspondence, 2012)

Macanese recipes in the public domain

'There are many excellent cooks distributed all over the world. It would be good to encourage them to interact and comments on recipes of their art (but communication should be done in both English and Portuguese), and to record their recipes.'
—Henri de Souza (personal correspondence, November 2017)

This call to action comes from a Macanese with a serious commitment to the preservation of culture, but is it possible that this encouragement for global interaction comes a little too soon, or runs a little too much against the processes of Macanese cooking culture?

The 'tradition' of keeping recipes to oneself has been materially changing. There are now multiple Macanese cookbooks published across English, Portuguese, and Chinese (and there are probably a few recipes translated into Japanese, showing up for example in guidebooks), though with one or two exceptions they have not been in circulation for more than two decades, and distribution often lacks efficiency. Recipes can also be found online (for example, there is a small selection on the official Macao Government Tourism Site),[7] but most specifically on the (public) pages of the Macau Library,[8] which lists around 200 recipes; sometimes a single dish with several different versions of the recipe. This represents a tremendous initiative and resource.

Why is the attitude to sharing changing now? In part this surely has to do with today's free flow of information via the World Wide Web; because of the dispersed, diasporic nature of the community; and owing to the ever-more global family units created as with Macanese increasingly marrying way beyond the Macanese-Portuguese and Chinese communities. Fundamentally, however, it is changing because so much of the knowledge is held in elderly sections of the population: one thinks of influential cooks such as Victoria Baptista at APOMAC or Aida Jesus, of Riquexo, who has remarkably passed 100 years of age.

The place for recipes

The ways in which the tension between local and global; between Portuguese-ness and Chinese-ness, and thus the hybrid nature that the Macanese themselves might represent, is perfectly illustrated on the Macanese Library site, where in spite of there being so many recipes in the public domain there's a caveat. 'These recipes are untested and many of them are incomplete, but they are included for historical reasons and also because they provide a basis for experimentation. I hope that people will report any improvements to me.'

This caveat contains at least two important statements for the purpose of this research. First, the recipes are important as pieces of social history. In the Shanghai Anthology, which was very kindly shared with me by Noreen de Sousa in Hong Kong (who also generously demonstrated some recipes for me in her domestic kitchen), we can glean fascinating things about the Macanese community, for example their

Figure 3.4: Portuguese olive oil, Fatima brand, especially made for the Macau market. Note the juxtaposition of Chinese characters with an image of the ruins of Sâo Paulo Catholic church on the can. Photo credit: Koon Ming Tang.

multiple identities as illustrated in language. The Anthology is typed out in English, but recipes include Portuguese measures (soup spoons and wine glasses); Portuguese words (e.g. 3 desertsp. [*sic*] *farinha d'arroz*; 4 sections garlic (*alho*); Chinese pinyin (½oz. Chinese celery (*insai*); 2 bunches *cheng choi*); and various ingredients suggestive of a certain cosmopolitanism—*champignon*, foam frosting, Marie biscuits, Shanghai rice, and Taikoo sugar.

Secondly, in many of the recipes in circulation, outside family circles but even within, implicit kitchen and even butchering knowledge may be assumed (for example, one recipe begins 'Prepare the pheasant in the usual way'); and weights and measures may not be specified. Chinese wet market terms such as *cates* and *taes* that are not in common usage today are often included, and sometimes an ingredient such as an egg or ginger is listed not by weight or amount but by price—for example, 20c. The latter suggests a stable society—and marketplace—unfettered by inflation or food shortages.

Such practices are underpinned by comments from Anthony Cabral:

> 'Our family recipes came through our grandmother and had odd references on quantities. My grandmother chose to say 1 cent of this and 5 cents of that rather than using imperial measures—leaving it up to my father to decode her references.' (personal correspondence, 2017)

Sometimes a decision has simply been made to omit a crucial or 'secret' ingredient—for whatever reason/s. Here is a quite innocent example of why details might be omitted: the creative nature of the cooking process itself.

'My daughter prepares a Christmas Empada every year and she used to follow the way it was done from watching a recorded video of her mother's methodology—her mother passed away in 2005, unfortunately. Well, guess what, whereas the recipe had the ingredients, my late wife kept on tasting and adding this and that until it was perfect and some of the items added were not even in the recipe.

This was also the case for Christmas Cake. My daughter has now perfected them both so she is able to continue with our traditional family lunch. I believe you need to watch how the Macanese food is prepared and cooked to finish with the correct product.' —Ivo Guterres (personal correspondence, November 2017).

Macanese cookbooks: For better or worse?

Food is used as a cultural referent and proves the existence of a community which is specifically Macanese, at the interface of the Chinese and Portuguese communities. (Augustin-Jean 2002, 123)

It has been argued that in order to exist or be recognised as a cuisine, a body of recipes needs to be recorded and then disseminated, preferably with the discursive support of food scholars, restaurant critics, and celebrity chefs (for example, see Wilk 2006, 159). The importance of the recognition of Macanese food as a unique culinary canon is reflected in the Augustin-Jean quote above; yet at the same time there's a tension with the notion of sharing recipes and demonstrating techniques. There's a further tension between the sense of local and regional, given that Macanese foodways also represent a global-fusion cooking (see Wilk 2002, 68 for his argument that the ramifications of globalisation and a sense of local identity are in fact closely related processes). 'Cuisines are not limited by geography or nationhood. Each national cuisine bears the traces of trade, travel and, increasingly, technology' (James 1997, 73).

Discussions have centred on the construction of the cookbook: see, for example, Wilk (2002). Taking the post-colonial country of Belize, in the process of exploring and seeking a post-British identity, Richard Wilk has examined the idea that if the country wanted to be a 'real nation' it needed, among other cultural identifiers, a national cuisine. How could that happen? 'Development meant finding and formalizing Belizean food as quickly as possible. Two of the three cookbooks published in Belize were the result of projects funded by international aid organizations with the intention of filling this gap' (Wilk 2002, 84).

Arjun Appadurai has argued that the proliferation of English-language Indian cookbooks has shadowed the process wherein people were moving away from their regions of birth for professional purposes and thereby experiencing 'another' India; if not entering the global diaspora. These cookbooks privileged dishes their regional identity, but by juxtaposing them with dishes from different regions allowed readers access to the cooking of the 'other' while embedding the idea of there being such a thing as Indian cuisine. He also talks about the demand from the Indian diaspora for such books, perhaps representing a nostalgia for a 'national' unity that had in fact had never existed (Appadurai 1988).

Mrs Lee's Cookbook, published in Singapore in 1974, is the subject of study for Jean Duruz. Mrs. Lee is none other than the mother of the 'architect' of modern Singapore, Lee Kuan Yew. It set out to record the art of Peranakan cooking—Mrs. Lee was born into this Straits community. But Duruz (2007) notes how this publishing project was part of the Singapore government's political project of embedding a Singaporean identity.

Publication of these cookbooks can thus be seen to cement cuisine/s, quite possibly as cultural construct for identity-building, and as a crucial narrative in nation-building/nationalising projects.

There is a certain irony that the recent emergence of a number of Macanese cookbooks may be achieving quite the reverse. This pattern may in fact be archiving Macanese foodways; the cookbooks are in fact serving as a historical recording of Macanese cooking, as opposed to representing a vital rebuilding or reconfiguring of the community. When presented in book form, family recipes may come across merely as part of a series of recipes rather clumsily and randomly juxtaposed. The sharing of food culture, even as this writer acknowledges, represents a most extraordinary entry point to a culture, and even a sense of inclusion in a culture, but can only go so far. So, then, it is the *reactions* from within that community to their food, their recipes, and to cookbooks pertaining to represent their food and recipes that becomes so illuminating.

Survey responses to the question about the extent of use of Macanese cookbooks

There is scant enthusiasm evidenced, and certainly no praise, for Macanese cookbooks within the Macanese community. Perhaps even the reverse is true, based on comments garnered during this research, such as: 'There are many Macanese cookbooks, of varying quality, and they are expensive.⁹ Some [writers] just copy from some old cookbooks... without acknowledgement' (respondent, personal correspondence, 2017).

Yet within the context of the actual survey, responses indicated that more-or-less one-third agreed that they used cookbooks; that one-third somewhat agreed; while the final third disagreed that they ever used cookbooks. Only one respondent specifically mentioned using the online Macanese Recipe Library resource.

'I use them, when in doubt of anything.' —Survey respondent

'No time for recipes from a book.' —Survey respondent

'Have one Macanese recipe book.' —Survey respondent

'I learn to cook Macanese food through family members and friends. Very rarely do I use Macanese cookbooks.' —Survey respondent

'Cookbook is more for reference only; rely on what I know or known family/friends recipes, if I am unable to ask a family member or friend.' —Survey respondent

'Only if can't get recipe from family member or friend.' —Survey respondent

'I only refer to cookbooks when I haven't cooked it for a while.' —Survey respondent

These kinds of comments thus indicate that while Macanese are using Macanese cookbooks they do so only rather apologetically or even disparagingly. Respondents noted that they might refer to the 'one' Macanese cookbook they own; or that they might only refer to a book if they have forgotten something, have not cooked for a while, or cannot readily get the recipe or handy tip they need from a friend or family member. Others refer to privately distributed informal 'cookbooks' and records of family recipes in the form of scrapbooks as their recipe source.

Why might there be this apparent disengagement with or disrespect for cookbooks, even as half of respondents are to a greater or lesser extent agreeing that they use them? The respondent quoted earlier, who had concerns about plagiarism in some Macanese cookbooks, also said that he had a good collection of Macanese cookbooks and that he also bought them for his children, as well as being in the practice of cooking Macanese food for his grandchildren.

The transition from a foodway—even as we call Macanese cooking a foodway recognised and practised within the Macanese community (and outside that community, among those interested, such as among Hong Kongers and global foodies)—born from family recipes that enter the public domain through publication of globally available cookbooks, complete with colour images, is clearly problematic.

Cookbooks can fulfil multifaceted positive functions such as to record and preserve, to educate and create new knowledge, and to democratize. However, they can also—much like myriad celebrity chef cooking shows on the television—actually serve to alienate a person from their culinary culture, moving it into a different domain. José Manuel Sobral has argued that the writing of cookbooks requires invention, recreation, and codification, and that the act of putting into writing recipes that were previously transmitting orally is about 'constructing a culinary canon'. This *construction* of cooking, he says, is in stark contrast to cooking that 'is learned on the spot by seeing and practicing'; and he emphasises that 'The distance between the contents of cookbooks and real culinary practices must be stressed' (Sobral 2014).

Might we argue that Macanese (and probably not only Macanese) cookbooks do, or have the propensity to, depersonalise, commodify, generalise, and globalise something that had stood as absolutely the reverse of that, with its emergence in the domestic kitchen and at community level? The family recipe for Porco Bafassa, held so dear within memories of family dinners, had now been replaced or displaced by a recipe that was deemed to be simply 'wrong'. The introduction of Macanese recipes into the public domain could be seen as an uncomfortable detachment of the ethnicity and broader culture of the 'producer' from a Macanese dish, resulting not in the new production of a dish in the kitchen of the 'other', but in a acculturated reproduction of a dish. The question is raised as to how could someone from outside the Macanese community; someone who has not observed Grandmother in the kitchen, say, or who could surely not understand the symbolism of, say, Minchi in terms of cultural identity, cook the *real* Macanese food?

Comments such as this one could be seen as revealing. 'Cook books are fine but still the interest in Macanese food diminishes because it takes a lot of time and effort to cook Macanese food which, generally speaking, do not come in small portions' (survey respondent). The comments of this respondent are illustrative of a lament around an overall diminishing of Macanese culture around food: the time-consuming cooking that fewer and fewer embrace; the large portions suggestive of extended family gatherings that happen less and less; a declining interest that could simply be about food fashions. For people eat differently down through the generations and young Macanese might prefer, say, to eat Japanese or Mexican.

> 'We are a dying race. Slowly we are losing the real Macanese recipes. People do cook, but they want healthier food, and there are all these allergies and intolerances today. Restaurants don't use traditional recipes because the food is seen to be too heavy.'
> —Isabela Costa (private conversation, October 2017, Macau)

Food and patua; food and writing

> 'My Mom and Aunts all speak Macanese patua amongst each other, but my Mom never taught or speaks it with me and has told me it was because she thinks it is a useless language.' —Johann Almeida (personal correspondence, November 2017)

The similarities between Macanese foodways and language—Macanese patuá—are often mooted, in the sense of their blending of cultural signifiers from several different places; and the Macanese patuá is heavy with Malay words. 'This unique patois, a mixture of mixtures, will fade out with time as it has outlived its usefulness' (Jorge da Silva 2015, 77). The use of the words 'outlived its usefulness' comes across as somewhat harsh; but the author precedes this statement with another, even harsher, one: 'Like the *Macaenses* themselves.' He makes it very clear, in his introduction to *Macaenses: The Portuguese in China*, that he is recording in English the history of the Portuguese in China before that history literally fades away. His work is clearly invaluable, but at the same time he has commented to me in private correspondence that few Macanese show much interest in reading his work. Books about the Macanese, then, whether about foodways in a cultural context, perhaps in the form of a cookbook, or books concerned with the broader sweep of history, are received with bittersweet emotions.

Conclusion: 'Season to Taste'

This chapter has begun to explore exactly what a recipe is and who it belongs to, even in a copyrighted sense. In the Macanese context, recipes talk to the centrality of family (which might also include the role of rivalry among families), and also to their relationship with place. It has begun to explore the different ways in which a recipe may be transmitted and the differing attitudes to recipe sharing, together with how attitudes may be changing over time. It moves to the thorny subject of Macanese cookbooks.

Jean Duruz's (2016) analysis of some of the functions of cookbooks—to formalise, to preserve, to educate the younger generations—may be relevant in the context of Macanese cookbooks. However, her assertion that Eurasian (her focus is on the cuisine of the Nyona-Baba) cookbooks embed 'nostalgic recollection' and 'hopes for the future', is unsupported if applied to Macanese cookbooks. Nostalgia may exist, embedded somewhere else; but hope for the future—of Macanese culture, of Macanese foodways, living on in the way that perhaps Peranakan foodways are seen to—has within this research barely shown its face.

When Macanese talk of their culture and their foodways disappearing or dying, there is perhaps the sense that there is a Macanese cuisine (and this could apply to any cuisine, really) that exists today in a pure form, when in fact it is more likely that 'cooking is in itself flexible, dynamic, and open-ended and, as such a practice of representation' (Avieli 2012, 246). How do people actually cook at home on a daily basis? Do we not, more often than not, prepare something based on what is in the store-cupboard, and what we happen to feel like eating in that moment, and thereafter simply make it up as we go along? Nir Avieli writes in the context of Vietnam, and quotes a friend of his who runs cooking classes in Hoi An: 'There is no correct way to cook Vietnamese food, there are only family recipes. I can only teach you what my mother taught me and what I like to cook' (Avieli 2012, 246).

Critically, the notion of the recipe as something to be recorded has been linked to the sense of loss, even death, wherein lies the depth and complexity of the form; and the complexity of attitudes to the recipe in which not only the death of the mother occurs, but also the death of the entirety of Macanese culture, right down to the loss of Macau, the place; the mother earth. To understand such processes, it is necessary to understand how Macanese cuisine came into being, and this is the focus of Chapter 4.

4

All at Sea: The Spread of Portuguese Culinary Influence across Asia

Human movement is a primary cause of changes in food behaviour. (Mintz 2008, 509–23)

Thanks to a combination of diplomacy, determination, and miscegenation strategies, to which should surely be added pluck and vision, Portugal seized the spice trade. The Portuguese took to the high seas and triumphantly transplanted the proceeds of this highly lucrative spice trade from the canals of Venice to the cobbles of Lisboa; and they were surely at one point in history the most important seafaring nation in the world.

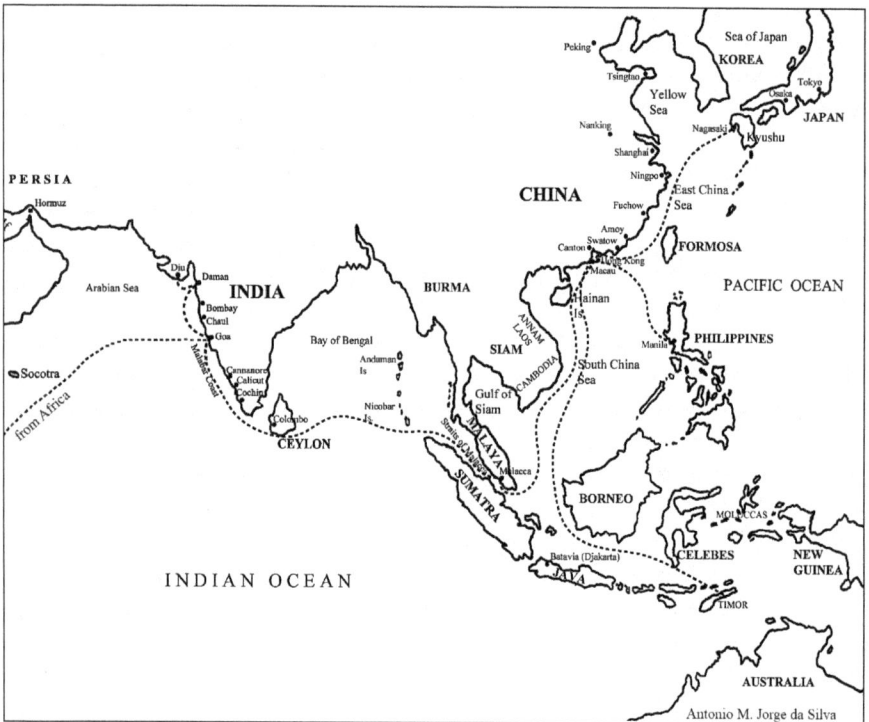

Map 4.1: Illustration showing Portugal's key trading posts and their geographical relationships. Courtesy of Tony da Silva.

Life at the heights of global power was short lived, however, thanks to the shared practices of the British and of the Dutch, manifested in their sheer brute force, economic prowess, and cynical colonial projects. In spite of this hegemonic brevity, the enduring cultural impact of the Portuguese in the wider world has been quite extraordinary.

Introduction

Portugal's culinary footprints in Asia go well beyond the foodways of the Macanese in Macau. Thus the emergence of these new foodways should not be seen in isolation, but needs to be investigated in the historical context of Portuguese Asian bases beyond Macau, and in particular their culinary footprints in Goa and Malacca. These outposts have in turn been influenced by forces beyond Asia, in the shape of agricultural produce and cooking styles of former Portuguese colonies in Africa such as Mozambique and Angola; and by the melting pot of cultures and thus cuisines in another former Portuguese colony, Brazil. In other words, this chapter explores more broadly definitions of cuisine and their influences. It examines not only colonial culinary elaborations in an Occident-Orient binary, but broadens out the discourse to include the results of the intra-Asia culinary exchanges that were simultaneously occurring.

Portuguese Culinary Footprints

In considering Portugal's activity in Asia, perhaps we think first of Malacca and Goa; and indeed Vindaloo, quite possibly the most famous 'curry' in the world, was created in Goa, India, by the Portuguese, combining Portuguese cooking techniques with Indian spices. Goa, today a popular beach resort destination, but with its cathedral and Catholic churches intact, is quite widely recognised as a former Portuguese colony.

However, the Portuguese influence went much further even within India, as Goa was a trading base—but only a base. In Calcutta, Goan cuisine, itself broadened by the Portuguese, went on to merge with the cuisine of the Anglo-Indians, and Portuguese-Goan dishes found their way onto Bengali menus (Taylor Sen 1996, 293). The smoked, salty Bandel cheese, which originated from a small town where the Portuguese had a settlement (outside the important port city Chittagong on the coast of Bengal), is still in production.[1]

The Portuguese were also active in the port city of Daman and the island of Diu, some 70 kilometres north of Mumbai (Bombay) and, today, about a twelve-hour drive from Goa. Mumbai-based chef and cookbook writer Zubin d'Souza, who was born in Goa, says that there is some Portuguese influence in Daman but not within the culinary sphere. 'The resident Hindus belong to a community of strict vegetarians and are cow worshippers ... Portuguese culinary-social insensitivity did not really appeal to them' (personal correspondence, December 2017).

Portuguese foodways do seem to have existed here, however, if somewhat below the radar. Dr Athos Fernandes has noted the consumption by the people of Daman of Portuguese dishes such as Espetada de Leitão during religious festivals; and also written of the daily consumption of foods such as 'arroz e caril, alh-piment de bombilins, sek-sek de camarao ou caranguejo, dal bafad, dampaca, xacuti, guizado de peixe ou carne, barrad de neutis, etc.' (Fernandes 1997, 231). These names correlate quite closely, or even exactly, with dishes found in Goan cookbooks, an occurrence that certainly suggests culinary conversations between the two places. The dish names are all rooted in a combination of Portuguese and antiquated Portuguese, further influenced by Asian vernacular.

For example, spellings fascinatingly vary but investigation into Xacuti (a curry with complex spicing) shows recipes for Fowl Chacuti (Fernandes 1990, 18), Chicken Chacooty (Reejhsinghani 1987, 79), and Mutton Chacouti (Reejhsinghani 1987, 96). Dodol,[2] a set coconut, rice flour, and jaggery dessert mentioned by Fernandes, appears as Doldoi (Reejhsinghani 1987, 26) and as Dodol (Fernandes 1997, 60), here with the recipe additionally incorporating cashew nuts. Portuguese dishes, or dishes influenced by the Portuguese such as Cozido and Val Nascido are mentioned on a Daman city guide website,[3] which also indicates there are restaurants in Daman serving Portuguese food.

Beyond India, and beyond 'official' colonies, significant influences are observable. The Portuguese first landed and set foot in Japan in 1542, and we can see that dozens of Japanese words in the culinary lexicon (and beyond) are borrowed from Portuguese: bolo (cake) is boro in Japanese; pâo (bread) is pan; and tempura was a frying technique introduced by the Portuguese.

In cinnamon-rich Sri Lanka, where the Portuguese arrived in 1505, a new model was developed whereby the production of spice, in this case cinnamon, was controlled, in addition to the trade, leading to almost virtual monopoly. Here, as an example of their presence, in a traditional Sri Lankan poem (translated by Shihan de Silva Jayasuriya) the verse runs thus: 'Drinking wine, eating bread / they came along the seashore; while walking, the Portuguese / sang these songs' (de Silva Jayasuriya 2008, 183).

In Thailand, Foi Thong is a match for Portuguese Cabelo de Noiva (Bride's Hair), though coconut milk replaces (then unavailable) cow's milk; and others, such as Loop Choop, resemble Algarve sweets, though they are fashioned out of yellow bean paste rather than with marzipan. The Portuguese had a settlement from 1516 on the west bank of Bangkok's Chao Phraya River. Links between Macau and (then) Ayutthaya were particularly strong, with the Portuguese community 'almost all in the hands of the established shipowners from Macao' (Halikowski Smith 2012, 85); and there are suggestions that Portugal wanted to strengthen trade ties, if not eventually colonise the kingdom.

Portuguese grape wine influences

Portugal's marked contributions to the wine world came about specifically because of its seafaring activities. Two out of the world's three greatest and most famous fortified wines, Port-wine and Madeira (the third being Sherry from Jerez, Spain) are Portuguese. Port-wine, produced in Portugal's Douro Valley, and Madeira—from the eponymous island that was discovered and became part of Portugal in 1420 (after captains of Prince Henry the Navigator were blown into the neighbouring island of Porto Santo a year earlier)—have enjoyed a distinct place in world seafaring trade.

Funchal, the capital of strategically important Madeira, became a stop-off point for voyages to South America, Asia, and Africa. Viticulture was introduced in about 1450, and white wine made from local grape varieties such as Bual, Terrantez, and Sercial, was included in the ship's rations. Barrels of wine would have been loaded onto the ships, also serving as ballast, and they were then offloaded at destination ports. On one trip to the tropics, barrels full of wine accidentally made the return journey to Madeira—their *vinho da roda*—and it was discovered that the extended rolling around on the waves, in conjunction with very warm temperatures, transformed the still wine into something that was different, but which tasted delicious. It had a sweet richness about it, but one that was balanced by a saline acidity. In 1794 the first estufa was created on the island itself: this method allowed for the creation of something close to the taste of the Madeira of the high seas, but this time achieved in a rather more scientific manner through a mechanised heating method. Madeira today is somewhat marginal as a wine, but it has its loyal supporters and today forms an important part of the tourism package on the island.

In similar vein, Port was originally a red table wine that was transformed into something 'other'. The British, coming from a country not known for wine production (though that has changed in the last two or three decades with the emergence of high-quality English sparkling wine), traditionally purchased their 'Claret' from the French, just across the Channel. But when relationships between the two went sour towards the end of the seventeenth century, London began to source wine from Portugal, with whom relationships had traditionally been solidly interactive. As an example, Catherine Braganza, of Portuguese 'dynasty' stock, married King Charles II of England (in 1662), and is credited as being the person who popularised the art of tea drinking in royal circles in England. The marriage was childless, however, so her influence ended with porcelain and Pu-er.

But the sea journey for wine barrels from Porto was long, and the wines were found to have become oxidised (that is, like vinegar) on arrival at warehousing facilities on London's River Thames. Merchants discovered, possibly in 1678, that the addition of brandy or similar high strength alcohol at source served to stabilise the wine, while also rendering it appealingly sweeter, and with (a probably appealingly) slightly higher level of alcohol. Business in Port became so buoyant that control mechanisms had to be put in place to, for example, maintain quality and stamp out adulteration. The sections of the Douro region deemed to produce the best grapes were demarcated in 1756, making it possibly the oldest wine region in the world (Chianti Classico and Tokay are also claimants of this honour).

Figure 4.1: Pipes (barrels) of Port are loaded onto a steam cargo ship in Gaia-Porto harbour, 2 miles from the Atlantic, for export, circa 1910–20. Photo courtesy of Symington Family Estates Archive.

On arrival at ports in Asia, Portuguese (table) wine must surely have been similarly maderised or oxidised, but it is listed as an item among cargos of Flemish clocks and Indian chintzes on voyages to Japan in the sixteenth century (Boxer 1948, 15). We learn that an 'honest wine-merchant' was operating in the enclave of Daman in 1854 (Fernandes 1997, 226); and it is clear that Macau has long been an important outpost for Portuguese wine. Little research has as yet been carried out into the history of Portuguese wine in Macau (or its position in Asia in general), but it probably accounted for half of Macau wine imports at least into the early 2000s, its appeal helped by the fact that it was taxed at a lower rate than wine from elsewhere. (Macau has, like Hong Kong, operated under zero wine duties since 2008.)

Certainly wine-loving Macau residents in the 1970s and 1980s would have been more familiar with the top wines of Portugal, such as Barca Velha (the inaugural quality bottled table wine from Douro, the first vintage of which—the 1952—was released to the export markets), than with Bordeaux-classed growths such as the aspirational Chateaux Lafite and Latour, the likes of which are today poured by the glass in the VIP rooms of Macau's casinos. Contemporary Macau is probably second only to Lisboa in terms of the breadth of Portuguese wine available on the market, and in particular the 'cult' wines are all there: from Quinta do Vale Meão and Neipoort's Batuta, to the wines of Luis Pato and his daughter Filipa in the Bairrada; the top-notch Syrah from Monte D'Oiro in the region of Lisboa; and wines from the fantastic Vinho Verde producer Soalheiro.

On a rather more humble level, that of Mateus Rosé, Hong Kong culture critic and restaurant owner Lau Kin Wai comments that in the 1970s Hong Kong residents would likely bring back a bottle of this after a trip to Macau. Mateus was once one of the top ten selling wines in the world, and this would have probably been the first experience of (grape) wine for most Hong Kongers (personal correspondence, July 2017). Indeed, as recently as the 1980s, Mateus Rosé was offered at even the most basic dai pai dongs (more-or-less defined as casual street food destinations where one could perch atop a plastic stool) on Macau's Taipa Island; and cheap Portuguese wine was (and is) even on the shelves of casual corner stores in the alleys of Coloane Village, alongside packs of dried rice noodles and cans of coconut milk.

The scope of this research is primarily in Asia, where the Portuguese managed their global and intra-Asian trade through a number of official and unofficial settlements, fortresses, and factories. They were the first Europeans to establish a colony in Asia (Goa, in 1510), and they remained there the longest: Macau was (at least nominally) under Portuguese rule until the December 1999 Handover, when the enclave came under Chinese administration. As a backdrop to the exploration of the development of Macanese cuisine in (and beyond) Macau, some historic context is required as to the movements of the Portuguese across Asia (and beyond) with regard to the movement of foodstuffs and food knowledge.

The Columbian Exchange

There is no less relevant place to start in a consideration of Portugal's culinary influences than with the so-called Columbian Exchange, which began in 1492 and continued into the sixteenth century. This historic process saw the discovery of 'exotic' plants, creatures and foods in the New World and their subsequent propagation across the world, the majority moving in the hands of the Portuguese (and Spanish). These agricultural introductions would do no less than to transform world diets. To their trading bases and colonies, the Portuguese introduced potatoes, sweet potatoes, tomatoes, chillies and eggplants, and maize and peanuts. Such were to go on and revolutionise not only diets, lifespans, and livelihoods, but also cuisines.

Christopher Columbus had been introduced by Caribbean natives to the chilli pepper in 1492, and while following its introduction it received a lukewarm response in Europe, it swept like wildfire across other continents. Within three decades, three different varieties of the chilli plant were already thriving in Goa, the Indian port city that was the Asian trading base of the Portuguese. Here, it was used as an alternative to the long pepper—a heating spice that is similar to the black peppercorn. The chilli pepper can be seen to be particularly transformative as it became an easy-to-grow, nutritious (high in Vitamin C), and flavourful addition to the most humble of diets, with its ability to perk up, say, a simple bowl of rice and dal. A South Indian poet even referred to the chilli as the 'Saviour of the Poor' (Collingham 2006, 53).

The Spice Trade

Exchange went the other way too. 'We know Europe developed an early craving for Eastern spices, and the Columbian voyages and those which followed had been inspired by a desire for a sea route to Asia to obtain such things' (Mintz 2007, 203). Spices were initially prized for their medicinal properties: the fact that they came from so far away seemed to bestow on them some magical, mystical powers to heal. They then became part of the decadent dining of the elite in medieval Europe, their expense bestowing prestige on those who could afford to cook with them. This liberal, lavish style of food was to be outlawed by the French during the Renaissance, beginning in 1535 when Catherine de Medici arrived with her Florentine cooks and a huge variety of fresh meat, fresh fruit, and fresh vegetables in tow (Clark 1975).[4] 'The sweet-and-sour effect formerly desired was now despised. They were in favour of allowing natural food flavours to sing, carried by rich, butter-based sauces' (Freedman 2008, 216). Medieval cooking would have had more in common with today's Indian, North African, and Middle Eastern cooking (Freedman 2008, 25) than culinary styles in contemporary Europe.

The discovery of spices from India being utilised in East Africa on his arrival there confirmed to explorer Vasco da Gama that he was on the right tracks, as it were. India was almost within sight and, with that, Portugal's imminent control of the spice trade. In 1498 the fleet arrived in Calicut, one of the great spice ports on the Malabar coast of Eastern India. A trade deal was struck: Portugal had found a new trade route that would go on to seriously dent the Egypt/Muslim-Venice trade partnership. Portugal had effectively stamped out the need for a middle-man. The ships went on to reach

Ceylon (now Sri Lanka) in 1505, home to the best cinnamon in the world; and thereafter the nutmeg island of Banda and the clove island of Ternate.

Having contextualised the Columbian Exchange and the spice trade, we now turn to an examination of Portugal's specific culinary conversations with its most important trading partners and colonial communities.

Portugal's Culinary Conversations in Asia

There is at least one glaring gap in our knowledge and that concerns East Timor; and perhaps not only East Timor but the broader sweep of Indonesia. 'In short, much research into Indonesian foodways remains to be done, and done soon, as food habits are changing swiftly, driven on by economic and industrial development and the rush of people from the countryside to the cities' (Davidson 1999, 400–401). Certainly in the case of East Timor, little would appear to have been added to the culinary literature since that was written. We do understand, however, that links between Timor and Goa were, strategically as well as geographically, distant, with the Portuguese who governed Timor managing to assume their own control beyond the influence of Goa. Links with Macau were similarly patchy, as Timor was not 'an area where the traders of Macau could always carry on a particularly lucrative trade' (Subrahmanyam 1993, 211). We can perhaps assume, therefore, that there was little opportunity for the trade of culinary conversation between the two. Portuguese rule lasted from 1702 to 1975, and Timor was plunged into civil war immediately after Portugal left, finally becoming an independent nation in 2002. It is one of the poorest corners of South East Asia. According to anecdotal evidence from a European chef long established in Indonesia, who visited East Timor in 2014, there is little culinary culture to note; he observed little more than the fact of the rather tedious daily consumption of water buffalo (personal correspondence, August 2017).

A second gap in the literature, and in our knowledge, concerns the Portuguese culinary conversations in Ceylon (now Sri Lanka), where their 'official' presence was from 1505 to 1658. We know much about the cooking of the 'Dutch Burghers', for example, the rice noodle dish String Hoppers and Lamprais (packets of rice in banana leaf)—though this Eurasion group likely had Portuguese blood in their ancestry too.

One country where we do have much evidence of culinary conversations is a surprising one, as it was never a colony but rather a trading partner, and that is Japan, with which a relationship began with the Portuguese in 1542. The Portuguese traded extensively with the Japanese via the southern part of Kyushu region (it is for this geographical reason, it is believed, that the Portuguese were known as the 'southern Barbarians'). They were the middlemen in Japan-China trade, and also began to marry Japanese Christians, just as they married converts in Goa and Malacca. 'Miscegenation of the Portuguese and Japanese women over the years produced a small Luso-Japanese community in Nagasaki' (Jorge da Silva 2015, 41), which would later swell the population of Macau.

Their cultural influence is apparent not only in the significant Christian population, but on Japanese screens that depict the aping of Portuguese dress, manners, food, and even, on occasions, speech (Boxer 1948, 24). As a result of relationships with Christian women, a whole new kitchen conversation emerged. Portuguese traders and Jesuit priests introduced bread to Japan, as well as the deep-fried, breaded meat cutlets known as katsu and, of course, tempura. Anyone who has tried one of the few notable cooked vegetable dishes in the Portuguese canon, the delicious and delicate Portuguese deep-fried green bean dish Peixinhos da Horta (literally: little fishes from the kitchen garden), could attest to the excellence of Portuguese deep-frying. The etymology of tempura is far from certain, but theories include that it comes from the Portuguese word *tempera* (to cook), or *temporo* (cookery). The word could also come from the Portuguese word *temporas*. These were the times, such as on Fridays, when no meat was consumed but only fish and vegetables. Perhaps it came from the word temple, an association perhaps with Buddhist vegetarianism, which is a particularly interesting theory given that the 'L' sound tends to sound more like an 'R' in spoken Japanese.

Portuguese-style cakes, the use of beaten eggs with sugar in cooking, and a general love of sugar, were also to emerge in Japan. Sugar was making its own socio-economic journey from being the preserve of the rich until the nineteenth century to being one of the first real commodities (along with tea) associated with Empire. (And of course the two, from opposite sides of the world, combined to create Britain's beverage of choice, with the addition of milk.) Perhaps Japan's most famous sweet cake is Kasutera, named after the light and fluffy Portuguese Castella, also known as Pâo de Lo.

The two places that seem to reveal the most about Portugal's culinary conversations in Asia are Goa and Malacca, with the latter in particular being significant within the context of the emergence of Macanese cuisine.

From Malaca to Malaka to Malacca to Melaka

'The majority of our [Macanese] dishes are a blend of Portuguese, Chinese and South East Asian cuisine and I have found some similar dishes when I travelled to Malaysia and Singapore.' —Marina Emam (personal correspondence, November 2017)

For a place with such a rich and diverse history and culture, Malacca (English spelling)/Melaka (Malay spelling, and the now correct and standardised spelling) had become a quiet and unassuming library-like city. But in the last decade, following its listing in 2008 as a UNESCO World Heritage Site, and subsequent government tourism initiatives, has noisily emerged as a tourist attraction. The city, the birthplace of an independent Malaysia in 1957, is about a two-hour drive from the capital city, Kuala Lumpur. Food provision in restaurants of dishes with historical cultural context, such as those with their roots in Portuguese cuisine, is increasingly seen as important for tourism: see, for example, Chua et al. (2011).

The Portuguese arrived in Malacca in 1511, where they retained power until 1646, and Malacca was the key to empire. 'At the height of Portuguese power the claim was

Plate 1.1: Picture perfect: Instagram-style take on Pastéis de Bacalhau at Café Encore, circa 2012. Photo credit: Wynn Macau.

Plate 1.2: Iconic soy-sauce flavoured dish Minchi. Photo credit: Koon Ming Tang.

Plate 1.3: Capela. Photo credit: Carlos Marreiros.

Plate 1.4: Empada de Peixe (Fish Pie), as prepared by J. Robarts. Photo credit: Anabela Estorninho.

Plate 1.5: Original Mateus Rosé bottle, 1940s. Photo credit: Sogrape Vinhos.

Plate 1.6: Current Mateus Rosé bottle. Photo credit: Sogrape Vinhos.

Plate 1.7: Tomatoes at Red Market, Macau. Photo credit: Cammy Yiu.

Plate 1.8: Cassia bark. Photo credit: Koon Ming Tang.

Plate 1.9: Pão de Lo, as cooked by Richard Laimbeer. Espresso cup from Macau is the author's own. Photo credit: Koon Ming Tang.

Plate 1.10: Lacassa, as prepared by Chef Antonia Manhão. Photo credit: Carlos Marreiros.

Plate 1.11: Cabbages at Red Market, Macau. Photo credit: Cammy Yiu.

Plate 1.12: Shrimps at Red Market, Macau. Photo credit: Cammy Yiu.

Plate 1.13: Shrimps fried with papaya flowers, as prepared by Chef Antonieta Manhão. Photo credit: Carlos Marreiros.

Plate 1.14: Diabo (Devil), as prepared by Chef Antonieta Manhão. Photo credit: Carlos Marreiros.

Plate 1.15: Porco Balichão Tamarinho. Photo credit: Carlos Marreiros.

Plate 1.16: A modern take on Casquinas by Chef Antonieta Manhão in Macau. Photo credit: Carlos Marreiros.

Plate 1.17: African Chicken. Photo credit: Koon Ming Tang.

Plate 1.18: Minchi, almost ready for serving, cooked by Richard Laimbeer. Photo credit: Koon Ming Tang.

Plate 1.19: Chillies at Red Market, Macau Photo credit: Cammy Yiu.

Plate 1.20: Fish drying in Coloane Village, Macau. Photo courtesy of MGTO.

Plate 1.21: Vegetable market stall in Macau. Photo courtesy of MGTO.

made by the pharmacist and diplomat Tome Pires that "whoever holds Malacca has his hand on the throat of Venice": "an appealing bit of geopolitical wisdom about the global spice trade"' (Freedman 2008, 204). 'The Portuguese put together a series of trading stations and fortifications that stretched from Brazil in the New World to Macau off the southern coast of China' (Freedman 2008, 205). Their colonial strategic structure, then, was not land- or territory-based, but centred on trading across coastal areas and port cities.

Malacca was under Portuguese colonial rule for 135 years, and they were to be superseded by both the British and the Dutch, with the latter 'exchanging' the territory for settlements in Indonesia. But even prior to Portuguese rule it was an important trading centre, in particular on the part of Fukienese seafarers. This section seeks to determine the extent of Portuguese influence on the cuisine of Malacca in the broader context of intra-Asian culinary conversations.

With the addition of Malacca to their empire, the Portuguese would 'acquire control of the monopoly of the spice trade' (Fernandis 2003), owing to the port's location on the west coast of peninsular Malaysia on the Straits of Malacca, one of the busiest shipping routes in the world (Ng and Karim 2016, 94). Indeed, it remains one of the busiest, currently carrying 250 trading vessels per day and one cruise ship per week. The port had been developed since probably about 1400 by the Fukinese and the founding of Malacca Sultanate, which is when the history of Chinese settlements is seen to begin (Ng and Karim 2016, 94). Historians believe that the Fukinese from China's Fujian Province, having run out of land to cultivate, expanded out of Amoy (now Xiamen) and went to sea (Wong 2003). They arrived in southern Vietnam (then part of the Champa Kingdom); at Indonesian islands such as Java; in Macau; and in Malacca, which has been identified as the earliest settlement of what was to become known as the Peranakan peoples. Penang and later Singapore would follow as Peranakan settlements, but with their own unique characteristics.

Like the Portuguese, the Chinese did not travel with women and wives from home; indeed, it was forbidden for Chinese women to leave China and travel overseas until the end of the nineteenth century (Ng and Karim 2016, 94). Thus, these traders with Hokkien and Fukienese ancestry began to settle down away from home and search for wives and concubines. There is lively discussion—in some quarters—as to the religion of the women they would marry. It is loudly whispered that the Chinese did indeed marry Muslim women. Lee Yuen Thien, manager of the Baba and Nyonya Heritage Museum in Malacca, further argues (personal conversation, July 2018) that there would have been Chinese traders pre-dating the Fukinese arrivals, who would have been required to stay there for at least three months because of the monsoon. Their own offspring could have married the 'new arrivals': thus the earliest Peranakans could in fact have been three-quarters Chinese. Lee also mentions that Buddhism and Hinduism were practised prior to Islam—the Hindu island of Bali is suggestive of this process—thus, the Chinese might have been able to marry someone of the same religion. The practice to marry and settle down accelerated after 1644, when the Ming dynasty outlawed overseas trade.

So, what to eat?

At this time, Malaysia and Indonesia did not exist as geographical entities, so there's a lot of shared culinary and cultural history; and even until today there are contested claims on the origins of, for example, Beef Rendang. As it happens, the origins of Rendang can probably be traced back to Indian merchants, though this dish has gone through several layers of evolution to become what is today known as Kepalo Samba ('head of the dishes') (Nurmufida et al. 2017). These researchers also argue that Massaman curry has its origins in India. The Kristang—descendants of the Portuguese in Malacca—also have their version of dry beef curry.

The Chinese trader immigrants, unable to cook the food of their home owing to the unavailability of produce and ingredients, began to reproduce their cuisine with the use of local materials. Thus, Peranakan cooking—also known as Nyonya and Baba cooking—has been defined as a cuisine that 'unites Chinese cooking techniques and ingredients, such as wok frying and pork, with Malaysian and Indonesian spices and flavours, such as tamarind, ginger and lemon grass' (Ng and Karim 2016, 96). As a fusing, should we define this cuisine, then, as creolised? Tan Chee-Beng likes to define Nyonya cooking as a cultural phenomenon, 'as a product of cultural localization', suggesting that the cuisine emerged 'from Chinese and non-Chinese cultural interaction in the context of the Malayan environment' (Tan 2007, 171). The consumption of pork will always draw a line between what is defined as Nyonya and what is defined as Malay cuisine, no matter the extent of localization (Tan 2007, 181). The eating of pork is also a distinction in Portuguese India, as we know from dishes such as Vindaloo. Tan Chee-Beng notes that although little is known of broader Nyonya culture, diners in Malaysia (and Singapore) are very familiar with Nyonya-Baba (Peranakan) cooking, thanks to the ubiquity of restaurants serving it (Tan 2007, 171). It was remarked more than thirty years ago that a revival of interest in the cuisine may just be a passing fad, or otherwise represent 'a genuine reflection of the vitality of Baba culture' (Clammer 1980, 118). It seems the latter may indeed have emerged to be the case.

In spite of the existence of a creolised cuisine pre-dating the arrival of the Portuguese, and the subsequent development of a hybrid Portuguese—known as Kristang—cuisine, a further point is made about the ever-continuing evolution of the Peranakan cuisine: 'Moreover, the cuisine is influenced by Thai, Indian, Dutch, Portuguese, and English techniques' (Ng and Karim 2016, 94). These Asian influences would be immediately evident in the enhanced use of chilli and fresh herbs (a Thai influence on the Peranakan cooking of the geographically closer city of Penang), and the use of Indian spices such as coriander and cumin. However, English influence may have focused more around etiquette. For example, a quintessential Peranakan china cabinet (reminiscent of an English one) would contain in equal measure Chinese teacups and rice bowls, and English bone china tea service paraphernalia; and the introduction of a set of parallel (British) dishes, or eating habits, as we similarly see in Kristang cooking, should be noted (see Chapter 5 for further exploration).

In Malacca, the Portuguese continued with their practice of marrying only women who had converted to Christianity, thus building a community that became known as the Kristang: a group identified by their religion rather than by their ethnicity (and as opposed to the Macanese, who were identified by their place of birth). Their history was not to turn out particularly favourably. Gerard Fernandis states that 'the Portuguese in Melaka started of [*sic*] as conquerors in the 16th century but ended up as fishermen at the lowest rung of the economic ladder by the 20th century' (Fernandis 2003, 286). Here he is talking about the 1641 Dutch seizure of Malacca. A few Portuguese Kristang were allowed to leave for ports such as Timor and Macau (see also Mamak 2007, 167), but many more—the Portuguese *casados* who had married local women—fled inland. They were not to enjoy the lifestyles such as those, later, of the Macanese in Macau (though, of course, fortunes did go up and down even in Macau). There was no push from Lisbon to embed Portuguese culture in Malacca; indeed it is suggested that these Portuguese Eurasians were effectively abandoned by the motherland. A journalist who visited the Portuguese settlement in the 1980s is purported to have described the Kristang as 'the bastards of the Portuguese Empire' (Fernandis 2003, 288). Without status as the generations passed, they were (and are) known as *grago*, after the humble seafood from which the fermented fish preparation belacan is made.

Tourism is helping to change their fortunes, and while some commentators fear for Malacca's future because of the pre-eminence of tourism, a foremost member of the Kristang community, Sara Frederica Santa Maria, who volunteers as a private tutor to young members of the community, has commented that tourism has given Kristang the chance to open businesses and a better chance of securing employment.

The Kampung Portugis (or Portuguese Settlement), a 11.5-hectare site developed in 1934, just 200 metres from the sea, for this fishing community of about 120 families, is now in itself a tourist attraction. There are a number of Kristang restaurants and cafés in the vicinity of Portuguese Square, from which the sea can be seen. Traditional Christmas celebrations held here also draw tourists. Even the fishing is now under threat, with controversial encroaching (non-Malay) land reclamation projects coming closer to the shore. Local historian Colin Goh, whose mother is Kristang, says that the community is 'always under threat—but it is very resilient. We have always looked to the sea—and now we have to look beyond the sea. We have to evolve' (personal conversation, July 2018).

Goh explains that although Kristang have traditionally married Kristang, or Christian converts from other communities, if they wish to marry a non-Christian a dispensation can be given by the local bishop in order for the marriage to take place in church. Clearly, there has been intermarriage between Peranakans and Kristang, and between Chinese and Kristang; hence there have been culinary conversations going on between these communities, which have gone on to influence Macanese cooking. Thus, though we normally insist on a palpable lack of Chinese influence in the development of Macanese cooking in Macau, Chinese culinary influence was already present through Peranakan culture, even if it was not initially diffused within the 'homeland' of Macau.

The case of fish sauce

Belachan

One particularly important culinary conversation, amidst layers of influence, surrounds belachan (spelt variously as belacan, blacan, belechang and so on). Belachan is a sun-dried shrimp paste most usually associated with Malaysian and Indonesian cooking, where the shrimps are pounded and then shaped into small bricks or balls. This condiment is fried or grilled before use until it is dark and crumbly, and its strongly distinctive aromas have been released. The heating of it may traditionally have been employed to kill off any germs that might be present (Tan 2007, 173). It is made from tiny, dried, shrimp-like crustaceans found in the Straits of Malacca, called geragau (grago, gerago). Belachan is particularly important in Nyonya-Baba cooking, being used in an array of different dishes, but it also forms the basis for Sambal Belacan, a condiment made by pounding fresh red chillies with belacan, to which salt and sugar may be added; and even a little lime juice (Tan 2007, 173). This condiment is almost certainly the genesis of, or inspiration for, Balichão, the aromatic shrimp preparation unique to Macanese cuisine (see Chapter 5 for a recipe for Balichão), where it is given a peculiarly Portuguese twist with the incorporation of, for example, bay leaf and brandy.

Cincaluk[5]

However, belachan may not be the end of the story as we seek to trace the roots of Macanese Balichão. There's another fermented fish sauce that is specifically associated

Figure 4.2: Cincaluk as purchased in Malacca. Photo credit: Carlos Jackson.

with Malacca, as it was born here, called cincaluk (cincalok). It seems to belong to the Portuguese period and is pre-dated by belachan. Such pungent sauces may not have been as alien to the Portuguese colonialists as we might think, given the use across Europe of the condiment garum and its association with the Greeks and the Romans. Remains of significantly sized garum factories have been excavated in Portugal and Spain, as well as in North Africa (Prichep 2013).

The liquid condiment cincaluk is made with a raw material similar to the geragau used for belachan, which are in this case combined with salt and a little cooked rice, then kept in a sealed container for fermentation for twenty to thirty days. A red colouring agent (such as tomato) may be added, as well as chillies. A Malaysian friend of this author, Ida Chow, commented that it was popular in Kuala Lumpur when she was a child in the 1960s–1970s, but that it seems less popular now (personal correspondence, December 2017). However, in Malacca it is widely used in restaurants and readily available, sold in places such as Malacca's buzzing central Pasar Besar Bachang market, as well as at roadside stalls.

Like Balichão, it comes in liquid form, rather than as a block. However, unlike Balichão, cincaluk is not first cooked and then incorporated into a dish, as is also the case with belachan. Rather, it is traditionally used as a dipping sauce, combined with chilli, shallot, and lime juice—recalling dipping sauces such as the Nuoc Cham of Vietnam and the Nam Prik of Thailand. It is very salty, so the tiny krill need to be rinsed in running water first. In Nyonya-Baba and Kristang cooking, it might be used in omelettes, and in Malay cooking in the popular salad comprised of sliced green mango, sliced shallot, and finely shredded banana blossom. It might be concluded that the Macanese Balichão is a hybrid form of (Malaysian/Indonesian) belachan and (Malaccan) cincaluk. And there's a Goan version, too, balchao, 'ballchow' also shows up in Goan recipes.

Rich with coconut milk and sour with tamarind: Food in Goa

> Cool sands
> Warm sea
> Green hills
> Gentle people
> No heaven this
> But must confess
> One may forget
> The need for heaven
> —Sadhguru, on Goa

The crusading Portuguese would have set out to obliterate the Hindu and Muslim customs of Goa; but under the shade of coconut palms and banana trees they ate unfamiliar local foods, and they ate these with their fingers.

The Portuguese began to establish themselves in India in 1498, and settled strategically on the lush, coastal city of Goa as the headquarters for their Asian trade. Their colonial strategy was, of course, less about divide and rule but more in accordance with a Catholic ideology to multiply—in this case with local converts. They married local and, according to a 1583 account by Dutchman Jan Huyghen van Linschoten, they embraced local food too. He was surprised to see them enjoying a rice and fish-based diet accented with mango chutney—a far cry indeed from the European wheat and meat-based victuals of the day (Collingham 2006, 54). Culinary acculturation was clearly well in hand; and according to a 1510 letter from Afonso de Albuquerque, the governor of Goa, to Portugal's king Dom Manuel I, 450 marriages had already been recorded between Portuguese men and Indian women, though not only in Goa but also along both coasts and in Bengal (Byrne 2012, 132).

Having settled in Goa, the Portuguese soon began a series of culinary conversations that began not with production but with produce, through the introduction of the chilli pepper, which was to feature very heavily in the cooking of Goa. The long pepper had been the key spice and had traditionally been grown there. European traveller Ralph Fitch reported on the bushes that grew in abundance without any need for tending, whereby the corns were simply harvested green and laid out in the sun to dry and turn black (Collingham 2006, 60). The chilli pepper soon became cheaper than the long pepper, and thus supplanted it (Collingham 2006, 53).

The Portuguese now began to create their own versions of spicy food. Vindaloo, a curry that went on to achieve world fame, is distinctive for its incorporation of red wine (and/or red wine vinegar).[6] It was created, as were all Goan dishes containing pork, by the Portuguese in Goa. '"Aloo" at the end of the name would seem to suggest that a vindaloo should contain potatoes,' writes chef and cookbook author Zubin d'Souza. 'The word is not Indian, but an amalgam of two Portuguese words, "vinho", which means wine and denotes the use of wine vinegar, and "alho", which means garlic' (d'Souza 2010). D'Souza is adamant that Vindaloo was created by the Portuguese, rather than being a hybrid Portuguese-Goan dish, since Goans would not yet be familiar with the use of vinegar (or wine, of course) as a marinating agent. The original Portuguese version, Carne de Vinha D'Alhos, originated in Madeira, where it remains almost the 'national dish' says Portuguese chef Kei de Freitas (personal conversation, January 2019), and is traditionally served at Christmas. He adds that this technique for marinating pork is still used in all former Portuguese colonies. When the Portuguese first arrived in Goa, they would not have had much access to wine, he says, so would have used coconut vinegar.

D'Souza further comments that Lamb Vindaloo is not the 'traditional' dish but rather a bastardisation of the original pork dish. 'Lamb Vindaloo never saw the light of day until Bangladeshi migrants to England decided to open "Indian" restaurants and added a version of the spicy stew to their menus. If you pay close attention to the recipe, you will notice that they cook potatoes along with the lamb. This is because they mistranslated the "aloo" part of vindaloo to mean potato since in Hindi that is exactly what we refer to spuds as' (Zubin d'Souza, private correspondence, August 2017).

The publication *Goa and Portugal: Their Cultural Links* is comprised of a number of papers, and is a summation of the proceedings of a conference held in Cologne (Germany) in 1996 entitled 'Intercultural Relations: Portugal and Goa' (Borges and Feldmann 1997). It contains some illuminating ideas, emanating from this, Portugal's first official Asia base, as to the spread of Christianity in Asia by the Portuguese, about Portuguese colonial projects, and about the cultural trajectories of the Portuguese themselves. The ideas of Fatima da Silva Gracias (1997) are particularly instructive here.

She talks about the transformation of dietary habits of Goans who converted to Christianity, such as the willing consumption of pork and of beef. As in Malacca, pork allows for an interesting if politicised distinction between Them and Us. The consumption of pork had of course been forbidden under the former Islamic leaders and also among Hindus, with its later acceptance among some Muslim groups carrying with it various political and religious manoeuvres. However, the situation is nuanced as though Indians did not eat domesticated pork, 'wild boar was fine when it was hunted—but Goa had the Bahmani Muslims who were hell-bent on conversions; and the Kadamba kings who moved folks back to Hinduism' (Zubin d'Souza, private correspondence, August 2017). There's an additional class element: d'Souza adds that pork eating was deemed acceptable among the lower castes.

The path of culinary hybridity was also being trod. 'Several Portuguese dishes became a part of Goan Christian cuisine which is a blend of eastern and western cuisine. Some of the Portuguese dishes in Goan cuisine were modified to suit our needs, tastes and availability of ingredients' (da Silva Gracias 1997). Her observations go further. 'The Portuguese not only introduced some of their food habits but also brought along Chinese food habits from Macau and Malacca' (Borges and Feldmann 1997, 46). It is an intriguing idea that there were Chinese food habits introduced to Goan society way back then, and this is certainly an area for further research. She goes on to mention, in this context and by way of a footnote, how 'many of our popular dishes such as Vindalho, balchao, caldeirada, cabidel, feijoaida, sorapatel, guisados was [*sic*] introduced to our land by the Portuguese. In a second footnote, da Silva Gracias also mentions both Burma (now Myanmar) and Malacca as being the origins of balchao. 'In Macau this dish is known as Balichao,' she writes. While unsupported (uncited), these comments about culinary exchange strengthen the idea that the culinary conversations going on within Asia, as well as with the outside European forces, were complex and varied, and should not be viewed either as systematic or chronological.

Zubin d'Souza has a similar idea as to what constitutes Goan cuisine. 'The list of Portuguese dishes in Goa also include Sorpotael which is a pork and pork liver stew, cabidael which is a tripe dish that originated from Oporto from the time of Henry the Navigator, Feijoado which is a bean and pork stew … actually almost any Goan pork dish is Portuguese in origin since they earlier had Islamic rulers' (private correspondence, July 2017).

In Joyce Fernandes' *Goan Cookbook* (1990), Feijoada is one of just a handful of recipes that don't incorporate spice or chilli—thus coming from a more Portuguese-European bent—though the list of ingredients for Feijoada does include Goan spicy sausage. The pork and pork liver stew Sorpotel (also spelt as Sorapatel, Sarapatel), is another dish that d'Souza mentions, above, and this is of particular note. It has been argued that this is a dish based on the Portuguese dish Sarabulho (da Silva Gracias 1997), whereas the Macanese would consider this dish to be central to their own canon. Recalls Marina de Senna Fernandes: 'My granny was famous for her sarrabulho (a dish redolent with spice[,] made from pig blood and chicken offal) and I was lucky enough to have tried it during my teenage years; but sadly, she didn't leave the recipe written down for anyone' (Jackson 2003, 28). However, the Macanese Sarrabulho is

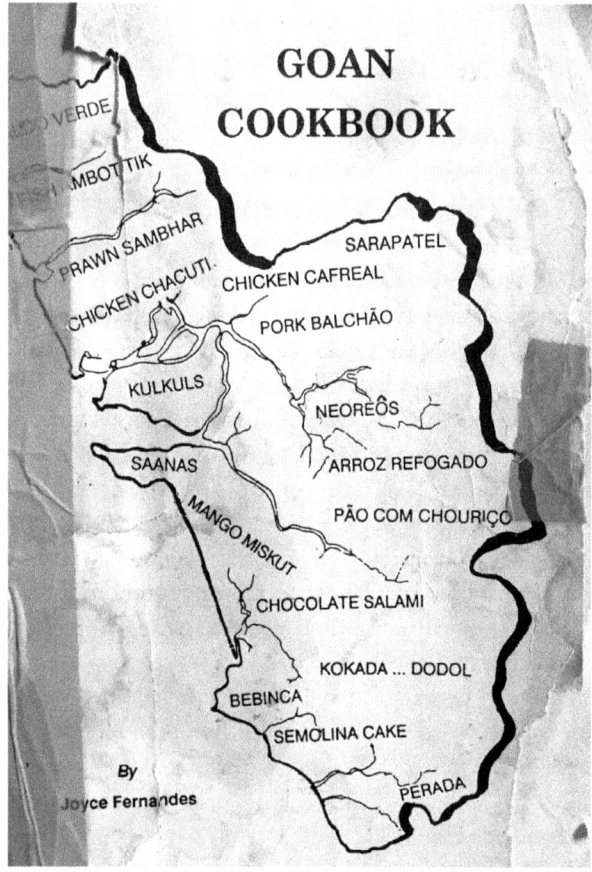

Figure 4.3: The author's own rather battered copy! Photo credit: Annabel Jackson.

most likely to be a version of the Papas de Sarrabulho and Arroz de Sarrabulho from the Minho region of northern Portugal. Sorpatel and Sarrabulho are clearly closely related and are suggestive of a process whereby Macanese dishes were introduced to Goa.

Or did these dishes originate in Goa and go on to be introduced to Macau, where they were modified by the Macanese? How might that process have occurred? We know that at least the elite of Portugal, for example admirals and the governors of the various Asian outposts, would have been travelling to and from Goa, and might just have influenced the cooking of certain dishes that they encountered in slightly different forms in different places. But who else was moving around Asia?

The role of the Church: Culinary conversions as well as religious conversions?

In addition to trading relationships, which also involved political and diplomatic contact, the Church played a pivotal part in Portugal's colonial projects; and cultural contact through conversion was also taking place. In his paper on the relationship between Goa and Japan in the sixteenth and seventeenth centuries, Takashi Gonoi writes: 'It is important to underline that Goa was for Japan one type of passage between Portugal and the Catholic world . . . the government of Goa promised the consideration of ties of friendship between the government of Portugal and the principal

Figure 4.4: São Xavier Chapel, Coloane Village, Macau. Photo credit: Amy Law, Little Stories.

daimyos of the region of Kyushu' (Gonoi 1997, 109–10). He talks of young aspirants to the priesthood who would travel to study in Portugal, or in Goa, or in Malacca, or in Macau, and might additionally move between at least two of these places.

During the years after the cessation of Hong Kong to the British (they took possession of Hong Kong and Kowloon in 1841; the New Territories would follow in 1897), a long shadow was cast over Macau. The tiny land mass, with its shallow harbour as compared with Hong Kong's deep harbour, began to experience great economic and political problems, and fell into an era of unrest. Consequently, 'a contingent of Portuguese troops was sent from India to augment the militia' (Jorge da Silva 2015, 103). Their arrival swelled the Portuguese population, providing 'fresh' Portuguese blood to enter the Macanese mix—but could also have brought new dishes and ideas to the Macanese culinary canon.

The Catholic Church of Portugal is not associated with, say, the asceticism of Buddhism (or even Protestantism). Rather, the names of rich, sweet, and eggy desserts indicate exactly where they were created and by whom: Barriga de Freira (Nun's Belly), Papos de Anjo (Angel's Breasts), and Orelhas de Abade (Abbot's Ears), to name but a few. In food studies it is also important to remember that everyone has to eat, so conversations about food while dining are almost inevitable, as different cultures found themselves being introduced to entirely new flavours, taste combinations, and techniques. Macau could have been pivotal given its geographical location—it was much closer to Japan than Goa was. Thus it was not necessarily the Macanese who directly introduced their cuisine to Goa, but rather those young men studying for the priesthood and who were moving around Catholic centres. Culinary conversations were likely emerging on ships, among the numerous nationalities represented on the crews, among the passengers, and between ships' cooks and those they were serving. A contemporary example of this is the restaurant Henri's Galley in Macau. Henri, who is (mainland Chinese) Cantonese, worked on the ships where he cooked 'Portuguese' food. On land, he opened a 'Portuguese' restaurant in 1976, where he cooked some of his favourite 'Portuguese' dishes such as egg curry; and was apparently subsequently taught how to prepare Macanese dishes. The restaurant is now run by his son, Raymond Vong, and is particularly famous for its rendering of Macanese African Chicken.

As we explore in the context of Macanese cuisine, Goan food has not stood still; it is not a museum relic dating to Portuguese rule. The simple, self-published, little volume by Joyce Fernandes called *Goan Cookbook* (1990) contains recipes for dishes such as Balchao do Porco (pork with fermented shrimp sauce) and Galinha Cafreal (grilled 'black' chicken). Both would be considered to be Macanese, with the former credited with Malaccan roots (Mamak 2007, 167), and the latter usually credited with Mozambique origins (see, for example, Hamilton 2008, 309). Indeed, while Cherie Hamilton writes that African Chicken was exported from Mozambique to Macau, she doesn't even include a recipe for this dish (which would be considered among the Macanese as one of the most iconic of Macanese dishes) in the Macau section of the cookbook *Cuisines of Portuguese Encounters* (Hamilton 2008).

There are many foodways and culinary conversations to be unravelled here, including the possibility that the indigenous cooking of Macau was being reproduced in Goa or that Macanese cuisine largely originated there by dual-way of Malacca. It can be considered that when blood is mixed, differently constructed, broader palates emerge, juxtaposing disparate ingredients in unique and delicious ways.

Conclusion

Portuguese culinary influence in Asia cannot be studied without reference to the Columbian Exchange or the spice trade, both of which indicate the extent to which the Portuguese (and the Spanish) were instrumental in changing global agriculture and in transforming culinary mores. The introduction of new produce has been more important, perhaps, than the influencing of production, but both are incredibly relevant in the study of the history of cuisine.

Portuguese culinary influence in Asia cannot be said to have occurred thematically and exclusively in Portuguese colonies (and in fact Macau is not believed to have ever been an 'official' colony, rather referred to as an 'enclave'). Portuguese culinary influences can be seen, particularly in the pastry kitchen, from Bangkok to Bengal, and as far away as southern Japan. Intra-Asia culinary conversations were clearly also going on—between Goa and Macau, between Malacca and Macau, within Malacca, and all across time. Macanese cuisine, to which we now specifically turn, is unique in the way it emerged, but may carry broader influences that have tended to be overlooked, and indeed in turn influenced other Asian foodways.

5

Towards a Definition of Macanese Cuisine

Tell me what you eat and I shall tell you what you are.
—Brillat-Savarin, 1825

Surely even Jean Anthelme Brillat-Savarin, the erudite (French) lawyer, politician, writer, and gourmet, would have scratched his head—as would any linguist were there one at the table—upon being confronted with an evening spread of a startling juxtaposition of dishes with names such as Lacassa, Chachini, Porco Balichão Tamarinho, and Minchi; with accompaniments of both fresh bread and steamed rice, and quite possibly Portuguese red wine.

Linguistically, the dish names bounce around in temporal dimensions variously between, for example, Malay, Hindi, Portuguese, archaic Portuguese, Macanese patuá, and even a 'made-up' word, that being Minchi.

In culinary terms, this apparently motley crew of dishes comprises a curiously aromatic clear soup called Lacassa (shrimp, vermicelli, Balichão, coriander leaves); the dry, crumb-like Chachini (bacalhau (or other fish), coconut, turmeric, chillies); the dark and brooding Porco Balichão Tamarinho (pork, Balichão, tamarind, jaggery, ginger, bay leaf); and a heap of something called Minchi (ground pork, ground beef, diced onion, soy sauces light and dark, and English Worcestershire sauce (Lea & Perrins—the definitive brand); and even incorporating fried potato cubes as if bowls of rice and baskets of bread were not starch enough). Taste sensations, flavours, and ingredients range from salty to sweet to subtle to spicy; from chunks of slow cooked meat to finely sliced fish to the freshest of seafood; from an almost familiar broth to the apparently most unlikely of flavour combinations.

As the above paragraph might indicate, the depth and breadth of Macanese food render it a complex canon of dishes, and thus the palate of the typical Macanese one of the most complex in its ability to embrace so many different gustatory and aromatic cues.

Unlike any other national group in the world, the descendants of the Portuguese have made a part of their cuisine the most varied mixture of spices and multinational style of cooking and tastes. (Jorge da Silva 2016, 51)

In this chapter, as a backdrop to the broader research topic, we explore the genesis, definitions, and evolution of Macanese foodways. It is not every day that a new 'cuisine' is born. The conditions have to be right for that. But what are those conditions?

> **An aside: The transformation of cooking into cuisine**
>
> Cuisine is not food. Cuisine 'is food transcended, nature transformed into a social product, an aesthetic artefact, a linguistic creation, a cultural tradition' (Clark 1975). Additionally, the construction of a cuisine can be seen as a national, nation building, political project.
>
> In the case of France, however, we can look at cuisine not as a political project but as a civilizing project; an intellectual project supported by discourse at all levels. It remains thus to this day, with the support of its Michelin stars, its essayists (not the least of which being Brillat-Savarin and the chef Marie-Antoine Carême), and its fine wine; it has been the cuisine against which all others are measured.
>
> It was not until the sixteenth century that distinct European cuisines began to emerge from the heavy medieval fare 'which did not differ appreciably from one country to another' (Parkhurst Ferguson 2004, 36). In France this movement, which reached its zenith after the Renaissance, was represented by the elaboration of the technical, complex, and ambitious haute cuisine, where the status of chef was transformed from artisan to artist and the sauce béchamel was king. Critically, what had been the lavish cooking of the elite began its diffusion, through the democratic space of the restaurant, to become representative of the nation as a whole, as a cultural ideal.
>
> The cooking of the French had, with some of the precision of science, become a cuisine; become codified. To complete dominance at the dining table, a similar process would later be applied to wine—first with the Napoleonic 1855 Paris Classification of the wines of Bordeaux and the subsequent development of the AOC system from the 1930s.

The Portuguese: Historic Landings in Macau

Writers and commentators have ventured that when the Portuguese docked in Macau's Outer Harbour in 1555 they found a place 'sparsely populated' (see, for example, Jorge da Silva 2015, 29). Was it, then, a place without culture? By comparison with Hong Kong, which was ceded to the British some 300 years later in 1841, and which was already a thriving economy, this statement bears some truth.

The Portuguese came to shore by the A-Ma Temple (which stands to this day, a popular tourist attraction, with the well-executed Maritime Museum fittingly

Figure 5.1: A-Ma Temple, circa 2015. Photo credit: Cammy Yiu.

adjacent)—a temple to the goddess of the sea. The inhabitants of Macau at this time were believed to be a few fishing families who lived aboard their *tanca* fishing vessels. They are usually said to have been immigrants from nearby Fujian Province who, lacking sufficient land to cultivate, took to the sea (see, for example, Wong 2003, 4). Their knowledge of boats would become rather useful to the Portuguese for ship repairs and, later, in the design and building of the unique *lorcha*, 'a fast European-hulled boat with Chinese sails' (Jorge da Silva 2015, 29).[1]

Certainly the implication is that there were no land-based inhabitants here so, with the exception of A-Ma Temple, the very first workshops, storage facilities and residences would have been decidedly Portuguese in style, but with colonial architectural tweaks (perhaps a covered veranda to provide airy shelter from rain in the hot and humid typhoon season) such as we see elsewhere in parts of Asia that have been under European rule—Singapore and Hong Kong, for example. Thus, early Macau would have looked architecturally European, rather than Chinese (or Asian), as expressed here: 'Which it is I don't know, but I am seeing a Portuguese city on the seaside' (as cited in Jorge da Silva 2015, 121; from Fr. Manuel Teixeira).

Officially no Portuguese women travelled on the ships or resided in the colonies; and accounts from the Viceroy of India (appointed in 1508), Alfonso de Albuquerque, are suggestive of the opinion that (Portuguese Caucasian) women would simply be unable to survive the voyage. There was a subtext to their exclusion, however. 'Above all, in order to colonize successfully, Portugal needed to integrate with the local population' (Jorge da Silva 2015, 13). Integration through marriage was thus encouraged by Lisbon, although the Portuguese traders and seafarers were only allowed to marry Christians. Priests and missionaries thus went ahead of the merchant ships, tasked with converting inhabitants of trading outposts. Further, sailors were often encouraged to stay on foreign soil rather than make the return trip to Portugal, their absence allowing for maximum space for precious cargo. They would thus begin to reside with, and reproduce with, local women.

However, the colonial project was to be different in Macau. There were few, if any, eligible resident women there to first convert and then to marry. Thus, the Portuguese would bring with them women either born or already converted within existing Portuguese colonial outposts, such as Goa in India, Malacca in (now) Malaysia, and (now) East Timor; and from countries such as Japan and the Philippines, where the Portuguese enjoyed trading privileges. There were African (and probably from elsewhere) slaves as well, who would have worked on the ships, in the warehouses, and other places, inevitably mixing in their culinary traditions—as well as their blood. An account from 1635,[2] by which time the Portuguese would have been well established, the population of Macau was 7,000. This comprised 850 Portuguese, 300 Indian and Malay sailors and pilots, and 5,100 slaves (mostly Kaffirs—meaning African). This number of slaves appears implausible, and more research is certainly necessary here; research not only to do with the kinds of foods that were being cooked and eaten in Macau and on the ships at these times, but how slaves might have influenced culinary habits, as they are said to have done in Brazil, for example, with particular reference to Feijoada.

The birth of the Macanese

The Macanese, then, were Eurasians born into Christian families: offspring of Portuguese men and women from various Asian and South East Asian countries.[3] Such intermarrying had been part of Portugal's colonial philosophy, to help them cement, through interfamilial unions, their positions overseas. But given that there were few Chinese living in Macau who could be first converted (or who showed any interest in Christianity) and then married, Macau became a different kind of project, with Portuguese and Chinese living alongside, rather than with, each other. And because there were few Chinese living there, the first offspring of the new Portuguese settlement, what are now referred to as the Macanese referred to themselves as the *filhos da terra*, the children of the land; they considered (and consider) themselves the indigenous people of Macau. In any event, even as Chinese began to live in Macau they 'had no desire to integrate with the Portuguese, let alone marry them' (Jorge da Silva 2015, 81), in the same way that any integration or fusing with culinary traditions was of no interest. It was not until the end of the nineteenth century that there was any significant intermarrying between Chinese and people of Portuguese descent.

Macau the Place

Macau is a peninsula on a southern tip of Guangdong Province, on the South China Sea, which includes a pair of islands, Coloane and Taipa, though these three land masses are now entirely conjoined. Taipa was only annexed after the succession of nearby Hong Kong to the British (Jorge da Silva 2015, 100). These land masses form part of the Pearl River Delta, with land on either side of the river meeting in Guangzhou (previously Canton), the capital city of Guangdong, China's most southerly province—and traditionally Cantonese rather than Mandarin speaking.

The term 'Macau' requires some explanation. The Cantonese rendering of Ao-Men (sounds like Oh-Mun) is usually regarded as derived from A-ma Ao, the characters for which are suggestive of the rendering of A-Ma temple, named after the Goddess of the Sea, and incorporate the sense of 'Bay'. When the Portuguese arrived in Macau, they asked where they were, and the answer of 'A-Ma Goh' could well have been corrupted to sound like 'Macau'. The spelling of Macau—as opposed to Macao—is the 'modern' and official government spelling, with Macao being the traditional Portuguese rendering.

According to Antonia Jorge da Silva, there was initially some farming carried out in Macau by the Portuguese on land at nearby Heungshan. But, citing C. A. Montalto de Jesus: 'In course of time, this prudent measure was neglected, the rural district abandoned, and the colony placed on a most impolite dependence upon the Chinese for provisions' (Jorge da Silva 2016, 17). In other words, then, save for kitchen gardens

Figure 5.2: View from Grand Coloane Resort over Macau Golf and Country Club, looking south from Coloane Island. Parts of Coloane Island still exude peace and calm today. Photo credit: Amy Law, Little Stories.

(Jackson 2003, 34), leisure game shooting, and some attempts at local fishing, all foodstuffs entered Macau through the border gate, which had been constructed in 1573 to prevent the free flow of 'foreigners' into the mainland; this required that 'all things relating to cooking, including utensils and the cuisine itself, were imported' (Jorge da Silva 2016, 18). This situation left the Portuguese community vulnerable for daily necessities, and the withholding of food became a powerful political tool exercised by the Chinese in their negotiations with the Portuguese (Jorge da Silva 2016, 17; Doling 1994, 11). Clearly the practice of the withholding of victuals as a bargaining tool became well known far beyond Macau's shores. As an example, Antonio Coelho Guerreiro, the newly appointed Governor and Captain-General of the islands of Timor and Solor, arrived in Macau in 1701 for a six-month stay. Stashed among his military and technical equipment were 200 piculs of rice.[4] This was purportedly 'in order to avoid asking for sustenance on his arrival in the islands at a time when there was such a dirth [sic] of this food stuff' (Boxer 1948, 184).

The Pearl River Delta was rich in agriculture on the land, and the sea was similarly well laden; together they helped sustain a rice-based diet comprising plentiful fish and seafood, with fruit and vegetables, and pork and chicken the favoured meats. The staples of the Portuguese diet, then, on which Macanese cuisine would centre—fish and seafood, pork and chicken, potatoes and onions, and eggs—were in plentiful supply. The defining Asian flavours of the cuisine would emerge as the aged seafood preparation Balichâo (see recipe at the conclusion of this chapter), together with coconut milk and turmeric root.

The Portuguese did not arrive in Macau empty handed either, being already heavily involved in the spice trade: the heady aromas of peppercorns, star anise, cinnamon, and cloves rose from ships' holds. They carried provisions too: plenty of the dreaded ship's biscuits but also bacalhau (salt cod), Madeira wine, olives and olive oil, and the garlic-and-wine-cured meats—still very popular on the island of Madeira today, particularly at Christmas time—which had already become the basis for Vindaloo in Goa. They carried, too, thanks to the varying backgrounds of wives and servants, the intangible cultural skills and knowledge across many Asian cuisines, and of ingredients that were not native to southern China. Dishes incorporating non-native ingredients clearly had their origins in faraway places, and intra-Asian movement of people would already have been spurning culinary interchange. Conditions were ripe for a new, creolised cooking to emerge.

It is particularly important to note that there was no local existing culinary culture, Hakka, say, or Cantonese; and Chinese blood would only much later make up part of the Macanese ethnicity, either because a Chinese had assumed a Christian identity quite possibly because of having been raised in a Christian orphanage, or because the colonial marital rules sometimes tolerated religions beyond Catholicism. Even when the Chinese did become part of the Macau economy, building sailing vessels, for example, they would return home (to China 'proper') at night, through the border gate. There was thus no direct Chinese influence on the cuisine except for the utilisation of locally available perishables. Works by British artist George Chinnery, formerly of Calcutta, who lived in Macau from 1825 to 1852, show Chinese street traders selling Cantonese snacks, cuts of meat, and so on: so the community in Macau would have had exposure to Guangdong cooking, such as street food-style steamed dumplings, soup noodles, and fish balls.

The Macanese have also historically followed the Chinese in their commitment to 'looking after people's health by way of the food they eat' (Jorge 2004, 17). Thus we find a dish such as Chau Chau Parida, which is traditionally made with pork kidneys and is served to post-natal women: parida means 'delivered of a birth'. The Macanese also enthusiastically took part in local festivals such as Chinese New Year, in addition to Christian celebrations. 'Until the 19th century Macao was just a transit city for foreigners and Portuguese from the mainland, and although the Chinese afforded the city its character, its soul lay with the *Macaenses* (Macanese) or "sons of the land"' (Pons 1999, 100).

The Emergence of a New Foodway

How do we begin to explore the development of a new system of foodways, and one that is not an adaptive nor a hybrid cooking, but one associated with a unique people with a unique culture? It is also pertinent to place the development of a Macanese cooking against the backdrop of Portuguese fare at the time.

The European tables of the wealthy during medieval times were decadent affairs. The spice trade, which was to be taken over by the Portuguese, was originally run by the Arabs, and had made Venice remarkably wealthy. Sweet elements in meat dishes, such as dried fruit and nuts, were a result of Arab influence. Ancient cookbooks feature Venetian dishes such as risotto flavoured with honey and almonds. For spices, the more exotic and expensive the better, with the most prestigious emanating from the mystical lands of far-flung places. A recipe for Pork Rolls would be a good example of how such ingredients sat together: they comprise pork with currants, ground cumin, black pepper, and ground ginger rolled in filo pastry, then topped with a sauce of chicken stock flavoured with ground coriander, ground cinnamon, and brown sugar (Black 1992, 92).

The following would have been 'standard Portuguese fare during the sixteenth century': 'A stew of chicken simmered with cloves, cinnamon, black pepper, saffron and a little vinegar and thickened with ground almonds' (Collingham 2006, 60). Alongside this dish we can now, for example, place the Macanese Empada de Peixe (fish pie), which is traditionally served both at Christmas and as part of the traditional Cha Gordo buffet feast: a selection of sweet and savoury dishes, both hot and cold, served together on one table at Catholic events such as baptisms and weddings. The whitefish filling is based on onion and garlic, but also includes turmeric and ground coriander; while the wheat flour and egg yolk-based pastry is sweetened with icing sugar and flavoured with brandy. These apparently eclectic taste juxtapositions would not have come across as anything strange to a Portuguese. It is dishes such as these, then, that might have reminded the earliest settlers more poignantly of home than the bacalhau dishes we see as being central to the national cuisine of the modern Portuguese.

What Is Macanese Cooking?

The emergence of Macanese foodways can be traced through a variety of strands: from *saudade* (the longing for home experienced by the Portuguese experienced as an intense suffering, as expressed, for example, in the mournful music tradition *fado*), through to substitution out of necessity or desire, neighbourly rivalry, and finally, perhaps, to another kind of longing or sense of loss: for the varied aromas, flavours, and textures of Asian cuisines on the part of wives and servants.

Food writers have transmitted variously created and communicated mythologies around its emergence. There are similar stories linking Peranakan food and family in which, for example, mothers are said to have factored in a girl's mastery of the mortar and pestle—heard but not seen, behind a screen—before selecting her as a suitable marriage partner for their sons. A story around the birth of Macanese might run thus: 'Sir' arrives back at the colonial waterfront villa tired and hungry from an exhausting voyage back from Japan, or other foreign parts, and longs for the comforting, reassuring, family cooking of his mother. He goes to the kitchen with one of his servants where, as best as he could, he has shown her how to reconstitute a piece of bacalhau by soaking it in water overnight. Today, he shows her how to prepare it in a stew with thickly sliced potatoes, diced green bell peppers, and onion rings. The dish is richly flavoured through the conduits of liberal amounts of olive oil and garlic, and is later to become a standard dish in this household: an essentially Portuguese dish but one cooked with local vegetables. It is 'Macanese', though it would likely be defined as a Portuguese dish in Lisboa. The meanings of these foods ran deep. One Macanese historian has referred to Macanese cuisine as 'the *soul food of the Portuguese settlers and their descendants* living in Macau and, three centuries later, Hong Kong and Shanghai' (Jorge da Silva 2016, 24) (my emphasis).

Scenes such as this are being repeated across Macau's domestic kitchens. A Malay servant is preparing a beef stew with dried bay leaf and rosemary, and perhaps bits and pieces from the kitchen garden. The aromas are acceptable, but she considers the gravy rather thin on flavour. So she stirs in the cinnamon stick she knows from home, and a truly original dish is created. Similarly, fried crab is deemed lacking in flavour, so a wife of Goan descent adds fresh chillies and tamarind pulp (for a hot-sour sensation) that, in turn, remind *her* of home (Augustin-Jean 2002, 122; Doling 1994, 56–57). Fish pie, made with a sweetened pastry, is imaginatively flavoured with ground coriander and saffron (saffron, incidentally, almost always means turmeric in Macanese recipes). In the absence of fresh milk, coconut milk is used to make a tapioca dessert.

Papaya flowers from the tree growing outside the kitchen door are tossed into a stir-fried shrimp dish at the suggestion of a neighbour; and everyone is intrigued by the cooking smells of highly seasoned tripe dish emanating from the house on the hill. One wife tries to emulate it, and her version is now considered superior. In other words, 'different versions of the same dish co-existed during the same period while evolving into new variants in another period' (Mamak 2007, 167).

As Richard Wilk has pointed out, 'One of the most subtle ways that creolization took place was by giving foods of different origins their own time and place within the total dietary system' (Wilk 2002, 78). This kind of interpretation may help us see how the Macanese have also appropriated Portuguese dishes to the point that Macanese might consider them to be Macanese rather than Portuguese, because of the new meanings given to them. For example, the everyday Portuguese appetiser Pastéis de Bacalhau is juxtaposed with various sweet and savoury dishes on the Cha Gordo buffet spread.

Macanese cooking is so often, too often, erroneously referred to as a cross between Portuguese and Chinese, even by chefs working in Macau (who should surely know better); and random Google searches suggest the same, though they might include allusion to varied Portuguese maritime influences. We have tended to view Macanese cuisine as being of Portuguese genesis with Asian accents, and that may well prove to be incorrect as well. We may need to work towards a more nuanced but more detailed definition in the manner of the way that the canon of dishes within Peranakan cooking has been dissected. Here is an example of that process: 'The first is traditional Chinese (Hokkien) food with some alteration, the second is Malay-style dishes, and the last but not least are the innovated foods. In addition, the Nyonyas are famous for their colourful and delightful kuehs (cakes or sweets)' (Ng and Karim 2016, 94). In other words, the Asian component may be a fully-fledged dish as opposed to an ingredient or an accent, even if modified and borrowed from another community; and the exchange may go both ways. Macanese dishes may have been absorbed into eating habits in Malacca.

Cuisines of Malacca

It is pertinent to pay some attention at this point to this culinary avenue, because not only was it an early intra-Asia cultural culinary conversation, and so might offer insights into other cooking traditions to emerge later within Asia, but its specific relationship with the development of Macanese cooking bears examination. The Peranakan community had already been establishing itself well ahead of the arrival of the Portuguese, and this community had created a cuisine that existed outside and beyond the indigenous Malay cuisine. 'This cuisine owes its existence to early Chinese immigrants who found that the local food did not suit their taste buds. As they were also unable to cook the food of their homeland due to the unavailability of the ingredients, they tried to produce their own food with local materials' (Ng and Karim 2016, 93–94).

What is termed Peranakan, with its synonyms Straits Chinese, Baba (the males of the community), and Baba Chinese, tends to be defined in terms of the settling and marrying of Chinese immigrants from the early fifteenth century with local women.

It is quite possible that Malaysian women were acquired as wives and concubines when the rules of Islam were less strict regarding marriage outside the community; or indeed that baby girl Malaysian orphans were raised by Chinese. However, it has been hypothesised that 'the heavily Malayanized Baba culture is a product of cultural influences, and cannot be explained by reference to antique mating patterns' (Clammer 1980, 100–101). Clammer goes on to argue for the idea of Baba culture transcending Chinese and Malay, rather than being syncretic; that the cultural therein is being confused with ethnicity.

We can take the Baba dish Ponteh Ayam as an example. With its use of fermented soybean paste and sugar it is rather Chinese in identity; thus we could say that it is a Chinese dish that has been appropriated by the Baba. However, its name is distinctively Baba and, further, it is the meaning of the dish that renders it fundamentally Baba. 'Ponteh is ritually significant for the Baba for its association with worshipping ancestors' (Tan 2007, 176). There are also cultural constraints on when it can be eaten: it has quotidian associations but is not suitable for auspicious occasions such as weddings. It is noted that this dish is also one of the most well-known dishes in Kristang cooking (Nunis 2014, 73).

Nyonya-Baba sits alongside the three key cuisines of Malaysia/Singapore: Chinese, Indian, and Malay. However, these three may not be as distinct from each other as first thought. To start with, there are a number of different Chinese peoples represented, with the 'Chinese' cooking having 'Hokkien and Cantonese food as the baseline . . . supplemented by items from the minor dialect groups' (Chua and Rajah 2001). Chinese food itself has over time been 'Islamised': that is, through the omission of pork and pork products when it is sold in the public arena. The Chinese could readily eat Malay food but the Malays, being Muslim, could not eat Chinese food because of the prevalence of pork and pork products. 'The Islamization of Chinese food is in effect a very simple process, for all it requires is the slaughter of animals in accordance with Islamic rules and the elimination of pork and lard' (Chua and Rajah 2001). Simple it may be, but it is not without its critics, who believe that omitting pork from Chinese food is to remove its soul; and that Nyonya-Baba food without pork just doesn't taste right.

Further exploration must be done regarding the extent to which the Nyonya-Baba cuisine, itself probably to be defined as hybrid cooking,[5] was to go on to influence Macanese cuisine in ways that would go beyond the inclusion of simple 'Asian accents' of ingredients such as tamarind, fresh chillies, and fermented/aged fish sauce. 'Nyonya food cannot be described as Chinese or Malay in the 'traditional' sense nor stereotyped as hybridized; [They] have created many new foods for family meals out of the interaction of Chinese and local Malayan cultures (including those of Malay, Portuguese Eurasian, Chitty and others)' (Tan 2007, 181).

Further, the work of Tan Chee-Beng raises a number of issues around Nyonya-Baba cooking that are startlingly similar to those we consider when looking at the nature of Macanese cuisine. These include the importance of food for cultural identity;

the lack of recorded recipes; and implications of the dawn of independence of Malaysia and Singapore for the status of this 'other' cuisine. These issues further include the changing lifestyles such as attitudes to housing, shifting patterns in family sizes, and the potential for emigration. Since the 1980s, also relevant has been the resurgence of this hitherto marginalised cuisine as something that could be registered as reinvented and commodified. Further influences on Nyonya-Baba cuisine from outside Asia—listing Portuguese as well as Dutch and English—are also acknowledged (Tan 2007, 181). Critically, just like Macanese cuisine, Nyonya-Baba was 'created by womenfolk in their kitchen' (Ng and Karim 2016, 104).

The descendants of the Portuguese in Malacca: The Kristang

What is locally referred to as 'Portuguese' food, though it is actually localised Kristang cooking, is now being served in restaurants in the tourist destination of Portuguese Square, which sits on the shoreline at the edge of the Kristang Quarter. Let's take a vivid example. At a July 2018 dinner at Monterios, a restaurant run by two sisters, Kristang cuisine was represented in the following dishes: Prawn Sambal, Sweet and Sour Fish, Chicken Curry Debal, kailan stir-fried with garlic, fried bringal, squid with turmeric, and clams with ginger and garlic. Two additional dishes seemed to have little or nothing to do with Kristang traditions but would obviously please crowds: crab with salted egg (salted egg being almost fashionable these days) and baby scallops on their shells, smothered in butter.

'The Portuguese have developed their own recipes that have made them famous throughout the country,' says Gerard Fernandis, mentioning in particular Portuguese Baked Fish, and Devil Chicken Curry (Fernandis 2003, 287). A recipe for Melakan Devil's Mushroom Curry is included in *The Spice Routes* (Caldicott and Caldicott 2001, 117), identified as having sixteenth-century Portuguese origins, and the recipe is based on a dish discovered in a little café along Malacca's Medan Portugis. Belacan is listed among the ingredients. The resemblance of Devil's Curry to the Goan Vindaloo, with the incorporation of vinegar, suggests its inspiration could have been from this port city; or that the Portuguese also introduced the practice of cooking with vinegar to Malacca. 'The Kristang cuisine, a blend of East and West, is very underrated—it should be more widely known and celebrated, as with the traditional Nyonya cuisine' (Musa 2016, 105).

The scholarship on the patuá of Malacca's Kristang community is extensive, particularly when studied in comparison with other hybrid languages that emerged from other Portuguese communities in Asia. Research within this body of knowledge would suggest that Macanese patuá bears examination in terms relative to that of Malacca. Both incorporate archaic/non-archaic Portuguese words in various spellings—vaca/baca, seccu/seco, diabo/debal, binagre (vinegar), and pimento—as well as Malay words and those from patuá. Such terminologies are revealing in terms of the nature of the relative cuisines.

Figure 5.3: Book cover reproduced by kind permission of Melba Nunis and her family. She is the little girl in the picture!

But what of the literal foodways, of which little seems to have been recorded in terms of this Portuguese-Malaccan community? There are a number of dishes that entirely exclude the chilli spice associated with Malaysian cooking, including Chinese-inspired soups; and Fish and Chips, Shepherd's Pie, Beef Steaks, and Pork Chops, which date specifically to the British period (Nunis 2014). Indeed, the last two incorporate Lea & Perrins Worcestershire Sauce. Fish Croquettes (Nunis 2014, 44) is specifically reminiscent of Portuguese fish cookery; and Potato Cutlets (Nunis 2014, 46) is evocative of a similar dish in Indian cooking, but also in Indonesian foodways. Kristang recipes incorporating items such as luncheon meat, corned beef, and tinned sardines are suggestive of global foodways, even global diets, and an enthusiastic embrace of modernity.

In a manner not dissimilar to the emergence of the Peranakan cuisine, which drew on a number of influences including Chinese, some dishes in the Kristang canon would be considered Malay and some Peranakan. Chef Melba says that among the Peranakan dishes that came to be considered Kristang would be Keluak Curry,[6] Pineapple Curry, Fish Chuan Chuan, and Chicken Pongteh—though the latter would be cooked with pork (personal correspondence, July 2018). To this list could be added the Peranakan salad based on cucumber and pineapple, which very much resembles the Kristang dish. Cucumber, recalls Chef Nunis, was the go-to vegetable when she was a child, and pineapples have been widely available. One (ethnically Chinese) chef in Malacca demonstrated a dish that incorporates 'old' cucumber: that is, one that had been left on the plant until it had turned orange. It becomes highly fragrant in this state. If you've little more than cucumber to work with, you'd certainly embrace different ways in which to harvest it.

Figure 5.4: Papa Vincent's Fish Cutlets. This image was previously published in *A Kristang Family Cookbook*. Reproduced by permission of Melba Nunis and her family.

Figure 5.5: Kari Ambila. This image was previously published in *A Kristang Family Cookbook*. Reproduced by permission of Melba Nunis and her family.

A 'classic' Kristang dish, says cook-turned-chef Melba Nunis, who used to have her own family restaurant in Kuala Lumpur but during 2017 and 2018 was working at The Majestic hotel in Malacca (she returned to Kuala Lumpur at the end of 2018), could be identified as Kari Ambila. The dish would typically incorporate various cuts of pork—bacon bones, ribs, belly—combined with green beans, tamarind, cinnamon, and a spice blend close to that used for laksa: heavy on lemongrass, chillies, and shallots. This could be seen, perhaps, as an interpretation of a Portuguese stew of pork with onions?

Another 'classic' dish might be the Kristang Kari Captain. Its genesis is also the stuff of myth: in spite of 'Captain' being an English word, the story goes that a Portuguese sea captain fell in love with a local girl, and this was his favourite dish from her repertoire that she would cook for him—so she named it after him (Nunis 2014, 82).

And where are the culinary distinctions of Kristang? Perhaps we should start our analysis with vinegar, the ingredient/cooking method so associated with the

Figure 5.6: Kari Captain. This image was previously published in *A Kristang Family Cookbook*. Reproduced by permission of Melba Nunis and her family.

Portuguese, and first demonstrated in the colonial hybrid cooking of Goa. The global curry Vindaloo single-handedly places vinegar on a culinary pedestal. The focus in this book is on the Macanese and their cuisine; but it is clearly a cuisine that cannot be seen in isolation. Let's take as an example a Kristang dish associated with Christmas celebrations, Devil's Curry, which unusually in Malaysian cuisines features vinegar.

Kari Debal (Devil's Curry)

Recipe courtesy of The Majestic, Malacca

Ingredients
3 potatoes, cut into wedges
1 yellow onion, cut into wedges
Knob ginger, julienned
2 red chillies, sliced on the slant
600 g chicken pieces (no skin or bone)
1½ tbsp salt
2 tbsp sugar
5 tbsp Chinese white vinegar
250 ml cooking oil
300 ml water
Sambal ingredients, to be blended:
20 g dried chillies, chopped and soaked in warm water
120 g shallots
25 g galangal
20 g ginger

> 30 g lemongrass (bulbs only)
> 1 nutmeg
> 6 candlenuts
> 1 tbsp black mustard seeds
> ½ tbsp cloves
> 1 tbsp black peppercorns
> 125 ml water
>
> Method
> 1. Heat oil in a wok and sauté potatoes, onion, ginger, and chilli slices over medium heat until fragrant. Remove and set aside.
> 2. In the same wok, fry the blended sambal over a low heat until fragrant.
> 3. Add chicken, stir well, and cook over a low heat for 10 minutes.
> 4. Add water, cover, and cook over low heat until the chicken is almost cooked. Add potatoes, onion, ginger, and sliced chillies, and simmer until the potatoes are cooked through.
> 5. Transfer to a serving plate and serve with steamed rice or bread.

Nunis comments that the key Malaysian influence on the cooking of the Kristang is the incorporation of the Sambal, and notes that a Malaysian Sambal could be very similar to the one in the recipe above but that the proportions of each ingredient could be different. Excepting the application of the Sambal, it is instructive to look at a Macanese recipe—also called 'Devil' and also served at Christmas, in this case on the day after Christmas Day. It is striking that the core ingredients are the same: meats, potato, chilli, mustard (here by the jar rather than as seeds), and, critically, vinegar (here in the shape of the pickles). The Macanese version is said to be termed 'Diabo' variously because of the inclusion of chillies rendering it even more or a devil on the stomach (Jackson 2003, 73), or perhaps because its yellowish-red hues conjure up visions of hell's infernal flames (Jorge 2004, 94).

Figure 5.7: Kari Debal (Devil Curry). This image was previously published in *A Kristang Family Cookbook*. Reproduced by permission of Melba Nunis and her family.

Diabo ('Devil' Dish)

This recipe originally appeared in Taste of Macau: Portuguese Cuisine on the China Coast *(Jackson 2003)*

Ingredients
½ roasted chicken
6 roasted pork chops
1 kg cold leftover meats such as roast turkey, braised duck, ham
6 cloves garlic, smashed
1 onion, finely sliced
Red chilies, chopped (optional)
Olive oil, for frying
2 jars picked ginger slices, drained
1 jar pickled shallots, drained
Jar grainy Dijon-style mustards
6 large potatoes, peeled, boiled, and quartered
Hot water

Method
1. Roughly chop the cooked meats into two bite-sized pieces and set aside.
2. Sauté onion and garlic (and chillies, if using) in a little olive oil. Stir in pickles, mustard, and enough hot water to prevent the sauce sticking to the pan. Slowly stir in the chopped meats, coating each piece with the sauce.
3. Stir in potatoes at the last minute and heat through. Served with steamed white rice and a side salad.

Worthy of further comparison is a dish that in the Macanese canon is known as Porco Balichão Tamarinho, and in the Kristang patuá as Kari Porku Tambrinhyu.

Porco Balichão Tamarinho

This recipe first appeared in Taste of Macau: Portuguese Cuisine on the China Coast *(Jackson 2003)*

Ingredients
1 kg pork loin, cut into one bite-sized cubes
1 onion, finely chopped
2 cloves garlic, finely chopped
Olive oil, for frying
2 tbsp Balichão, ready fried
2 tbsp dark soy sauce

150 g tamarind pulp, soaked in 225 ml hot water, then strained
85 g palm sugar (or dark brown sugar)
325 ml boiling water

Method
1. Sauté onion and garlic in a little olive oil until soft. Add Balichão and continue cooking until well blended.
2. Combine diced pork and soy sauce, add to pot, and stir well. Add tamarind liquid, sugar, and boiling water. Cover and simmer for about 45 minutes until the pork is tender and the sauce thick.

The ingredients for the Kristang version of this sweet and sour dish are almost entirely identical—except for the addition of chillies and some turmeric (Nunis 2014, 74). A similar story can be observed in Goa, in *Goan Cookbook* (Fernandes 1990), with a dish called Balchao do Porco. Pork, onions, fat (or ghee), tomato ketchup, and 'balchao preserve' are the key ingredients, but the following are ground with vinegar: dried red chillies, cumin seeds, peppercorns, cinnamon and cloves, and fresh turmeric, ginger, and garlic. The similarities of this dish to the Macanese and Kristang versions are striking.

There is little consensus within the Macanese community itself as to what exactly constitutes Macanese cuisine. Macanese writer and researcher Antonio Jorge da Silva, a former lighting designer, asserts this is because 'some families in Macau have closer ethnic ties to Portugal than do others: many mainland Portuguese have married into

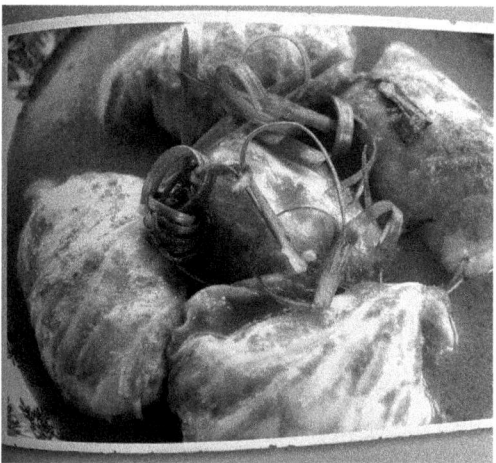

Figure 5.8: To name a few further examples, both Macanese and Kristang cuisines stuff cabbage leaves with ground pork (or chicken, for a modern halal version in Malacca). This image was previously published in *A Kristang Family Cookbook*. Reproduced by permission of Melba Nunis and her family.

Figure 5.9: Kristang version of Casquinas. This image was previously published in *A Kristang Family Cookbook*. Reproduced by permission of Melba Nunis and her family.

local *Macaense* families. This has a direct impact on the culinary preferences ... [and] some mainland traditional dishes have been integrated in *Macaense* cuisine' (Jackson 2003, 30). Other researchers have taken the question further, temporally. 'The development of Macanese food is fraught with ambiguities and dissonant voices and views. Macanese food is constantly reconfigured by different actors, at the imagined and material level in response to the tension between the discursive narratives and practical enactment' (Zhang and Pang 2012, 939).

Linguistic nuances in the definition of Macanese cuisine

There are linguistic complications in the search of a definition of Macanese cooking too. Within the Chinese language, the people referred to as Macanese, or the food referred to as Macanese, do not 'exist'. While in English the term 'Macanese' (or, in Portuguese, Macaense) refers to a specific people and a specific cuisine, '[T]he Chinese attribute the term Macanese to everything found in the territory' (Augustin-Jean 2002, 123).[7] 'Although they are often unable to identify Macanese food, they still call themselves Macanese and justify it by the fact that they live in the territory. Consequently, it is probable that the associations of the following terms are made by the Chinese population: Macanese food equals food of Macau (regardless of origin)/Macanese population equals inhabitants of Macau' (Augustin-Jean 2002, 123).

The question can certainly be raised as to whether this linguistic cul-de-sac denies the idea of there being a non-Chinese indigenous people in Macau and of there being a non-Chinese-based cuisine in Greater China. The identity question was further nuanced at the time of Handover in 1999. Portuguese of mixed blood born in Macau were referred to, in Cantonese, as 'natives' (*tusheng* 土生). After Handover, Chinese who had been born in Macau, or who had lived in Macau for a considerable period, themselves assumed the term 'native'—to distinguish themselves from mainland Chinese.[8] The Macanese people then became referred to as 'Portuguese natives' (*tusheng puren* 土生葡人) which, interestingly, is how the descendants of the Portuguese are referred to in Malacca, though in markedly different circumstances. 'Despite being cut-off from Portugal for almost 500 years and despite its assimilation of various local cultures, the public still refers to members of the Cristang [*sic*] as "Portuguese"' (as cited in Mamak 2007, 163).

Macau resident Patricia Lobo, who is Macanese, interprets the process in Macau thus. 'They are changing our identity—and now they are also changing our food. You can modernize Macanese food—but you don't reinvent it.' She cites Bacalhau Risotto as an (unwelcome) example of reinvention, which appears on the menu of a restaurant in Macau. 'Culturally, we were quiet but now we need to speak out, otherwise we will be "condemned" and our identity will disappear.' We might see, here, a need to believe in the 'purity' of Macanese cuisine in the face of its loss; to utilise food as 'a fluid symbolic medium for making statements about identity' (James 1997, 74). In fact, it has always been (as have most cuisines) in a state of flux, and not only as a result of the forces of modernity. As Allison James has put it, 'Each national cuisine bears the traces of trade, travel and, increasingly, of technology, so that food could more correctly be said to be constitutive of global rather than local cultures' (James 1997, 73).

Patricia Lobo sees the Macanese cultural identity as already being rather fragile, using the Portuguese expression 'Não é carne nem é peixe' to describe it. I asked Paulo Pinto, who works for IVDP (Institute of Douro Wine and Port) in Porto, who also happens to be a food writer, how we might best unpack this phrase. It means something like 'It's not meat nor fish'; or 'neither fish nor fowl' in more colloquial English. He responded thus: 'It's difficult to translate, but when put into action, you could translate it as "in the middle of nowhere". It can have the potential for everything or nothing' (private correspondence, December 2017).

Patricia talked about the idea of the Chinese feeling 'shame' about the Eurocentric nature of the history of Macau, and about why the Portuguese had managed to, or been allowed to, stay there over centuries (private conversation, Macau, October 2017). That the majority of the global population has not even heard of Macau (at least in this author's experience) further challenges a sense of belonging to a physical place and the idea of a stable, rooted identity.

Macanese Food Consumption in the Broader Context of Macanese Culture

There is little recorded history of Macau culinary culture. Thus: 'It is not easy to describe reliably and accurately what used to be served at the table of our Macanese forebears or what people once at as their "daily bread" in Macau's early days' (Jorge 2004, 7). We have a canon of recipes today, but dozens or even hundreds of dishes could have been forgotten. As Jorge points out, among others, more is known about what the English and Americans ate in Macau in the nineteenth century thanks to diaries such as those recorded by Harriett Low (2002). Much of what is known has been information gleaned by those elderly Macanese who have worked as private chefs, or in hotels and restaurants.

However, in *Macaenses: The Portuguese in China*, author Antonio Jorge da Silva cites (in his own translation from the Portuguese) Fr. Teixeira, who in *Macau no Seculo XVIII* indicates that eating habits were rather European in nature, complete with silver forks and tall wine glasses, and only fish on Fridays. Jorge da Silva writes: 'There is some reference to food preferences and habits in Ta-Si-Yang-Kuo, Vol. 1 and possibly other books written in Portuguese' (personal correspondence, January 2018). However, the practice of serving several dishes simultaneously, from which diners help themselves, could be seen to more closely mirror Asian and Chinese practices, as opposed to Portuguese or European traditions.

Macanese cooking can be very time consuming (and expensive), both in terms of gathering and preparing ingredients. Families were large and guests were often invited to share a meal, so elaborate preparation was justified, particularly for special occasions. The dessert called Bebinca (rice flour, sugar, egg yolk, coconut milk, and dairy milk) is left to rest for a whole day before it is baked; while the sweetmeat Talangko de Jagra, which is prepared for Chinese New Year, is only ready to eat after two days. Macanese Roast Soup requires cooking the meats for three hours before removing the meat from the bones, baking it in the oven, and only finally combining it with the soup preparation. Bolo Menino, a cake prepared with grated coconut and almonds, requires someone to beat twenty eggs, which, in the days before electricity, would have been a time-consuming task. The late lawyer and novelist Henrique de Senna Fernandes implied that in his family's kitchen there was one member of staff tasked only with the beating of eggs (personal conversation 1994).

Such details are provided in the Anthology of recipes previously (or perhaps still) circulating in the Macanese community of Hong Kong, by way of Shanghai. Further examination shows that the method for some recipes covers an entire sheet of A4 from the manual typewriter, suggesting the enviable time once available to be spent in the kitchen (or the availability of servants). Others start with flamboyant phrases such as: 'Prepare the pheasant in the usual way' (hunting for wild game and birds was a popular pastime in the woodlands on Taipa island); and one recipe begins with instructions for the butcher when buying a sheep's head, and what to do with it when you get it home.

According to general personal observation, but also based on the findings of this research, it is clear that fewer and fewer Macanese cook at home any longer, but family gatherings such as baptisms and weddings are big occasions when the traditional Cha Gordo is served. This is a series of dishes cooked for celebrations and presented buffet style, with often bite-sized sweet and savoury dishes sharing the table. Dishes include Chamussas (stuffed pastries, deep-fried), Minchi (see elsewhere in this chapter for the recipe), Ade Cabidela (duck cooked in its own blood, a variation of the Portuguese chicken cooked in its own blood), Porco Balichão Tamarinho (a salty and sour pork braise), Arroz Gordo (literally 'Fat Rice'—meats layered with rice), Mango Pudding (distinguishable from the Cantonese version as its contains chopped pieces of fruit), and Bagi (rice pudding made with coconut milk). Since this is a standing buffet, nothing served requires a knife for cutting.

This centrality of Macanese foodways to Macanese cultural identify has revealed itself in some interesting ways. It has often been mooted that the lack of Macanese restaurants (the first, Riquexo, opened as recently as 1978) is because this is not a restaurant food as it was created in the domestic kitchens, where aesthetics were rarely if ever given consideration. The question might be asked as to whether Macanese simply wanted to keep their cooking within their own community. Until the 1990s almost nothing had been written about Macanese food, and recipes were almost exclusively handed down orally and only within families. Sometimes they were not handed down at all. Comment is made about recipes 'whispered into the ear of a younger family member before being recorded on paper and duly "interpreted" by their descendants' (Jorge 2004, 24). One handwritten recipe found contains a diagram showing how to wrap a pastry triangle. It is written on a Hong Kong hospital notepad.

'It is quite possible that the best recipes for each special delicacy has [sic] gone to the grave along with the people famous in their day for their culinary arts' (Jorge 2004, 10). Restaurateurs such as Isabel Eusebio (Balichão) and Sonia Palmer (Riquexo) were concerned that the cuisine was dying out and began to share recipes and ideas. It was still being cooked well, but by an increasingly older group of mostly women (such as Isabel's mother, Maria Eusebio, and Sonia's mother, Aida Jesus), who were becoming too elderly to continue. With increasing interest in world cooking and cultural tourism emerging, Macanese cuisine caught the wave, and about fifteen years ago books began to be published about Macau and the place of Macanese cuisine therein, in several languages.

The secrets contained within recipes as regards cultural identity, and even contained in their names, are a focus for Macanese writer Cecilia Jorge. 'Rather than strive to determine what is or not Portuguese heritage among the delicacies we still so enjoy today, we should try to "read" between the recipe lines,' she writes in the introduction to *Macanese Cooking* (Jorge 200, 8). 'We should take note of the names (or various names) of the dish, its native and foreign ingredients, how it is prepared, cooked and when it is served. From this "reading" we can form a notion as to our collective identity.' We're looking at something akin to anthropologist Clifford Geertz's so-called 'thick description'—replacing a merely factual representation with an interpretative structure.

For many of the words contained in the names of Macanese dishes are not Portuguese, but Malay, or from the patuá. Maria Eusebio contributes a helpful observation here, from another cultural domain, and that is Macanese theatre, when she first watched the Doci Papiacm di Macau at the Macau Cultural Centre in 2001, a company which performs in Macanese patuá, with her mother. 'Only at that moment did I realise that I actually understood the language, without having heard it spoken explicitly before. It was then that I came to know certain phrases or words that my Macanese relatives spoke were actually patuá and not formal Portuguese' (Eusebio 2013). Further, many words from this creolised language that became dish names were based on archaic Portuguese and, as has been pointed out, from 'another' language 'used by Portuguese soldiers with little education during the Portuguese voyages of discovery' (Jorge da Silva 2015, 31).

Cecilia Jorge concludes: 'Macanese miscegenation is, in cultural terms, the result of a process still in transformation and at different rhythms as set by historical events' (Jorge 2004, 8). There is no one recipe, no perfect recipe, and everything is in a state of flux.

Recipes that have been circulated previously, for example among the Macanese community in Hong Kong, are illuminating. The aforementioned Anthology, typed on a manual typewriter and amounting to more than 100 pages, gathered recipes from Macanese all over the world. Historian Tony da Silva places it as having come from Shanghai in the 1930s. It is possible that this anthology represented the first time that Macanese recipes had been recorded in the community, public domain, beyond the confines of the family, and is when what was cooked at home by Macanese families began to assume a broader, public role as a marker of identity.

The editor credits many of the recipes with names (Guilly appears most frequently; Delmira Alves is sometimes D.A.; and one recipe is from 'Melita's cook, Adi'). Where more than one recipe for the same dish is included, the editor might comment on which one appears better or more authentic. For some recipes, the detail provided is impressive: these recipes are not about purposely leaving out detail. 'Do not leave in a draught. These Itena Podre should be absolutely white so be careful not to brown them at all. No lard at all is needed.' And for Sonho Recheado: 'One hand kneading is enough. Just roll your hand round and round on the pastry. When it sticks too much on the board, scrape the board with a knife and put all the dough in a pile.' In others there is no method given, but our editor-typist generously shares her/his own suggestions.

The presentation of the recipes indicates the travelled and cosmopolitan nature of the community, and they are presented in English. However, Cantonese ingredients are typed in pinyin: such as 'lap cheong' (Chinese sausage) and 'kai choi' (Cantonese bitter vegetables). Ingredients such as rice flour and white wine are listed in Portuguese (farina [sic] arroz pulu, vinho branco) or in both English and Portuguese (turnip/

rabono and garlic/alho). One recipe converts ounces to catties—the catty being the traditional measurement in a Cantonese market (1 catty = 22 ounces). Measurements might be in (Portuguese) coffee spoons rather than teaspoons, and soup spoons rather than tablespoons; and some ingredients, such as ginger, are listed not by weight or by size but by cost: 20c. Prices were clearly stable, and inflation was not a consideration.

Macanese foodways: The embodiment of Macanese culture?

Macanese 'cuisine' assumes a central position in the debate in Macau as to whether a new and separate culture did—and does—exist. 'Food is used as a cultural referent and *proves the existence of a community* which is specifically Macanese, at the interface of the Chinese and Portuguese communities' (Augustin-Jean 2002, 123) (my emphasis). Although we can assume that Macanese foodways slowly became embedded through oral transmission of recipes, there is scant recorded information of this process: further evidence that the Chinese community were somewhat dismissive of it; and any Portuguese records from the sixteenth and seventeenth centuries have been lost (Braga 2012).

Certainly, the Chinese did not actively and creatively engage with this emerging cooking culture, in the way that the Goans, the Malaccans, and the Japanese did; and there are even no records of the foodstuffs imported into Macau across history. 'As in many other cultures whose past was mainly recorded down by people not at all interested in preserving the traditions of its indigenous or local people, accounts on early Macanese cuisine are hard to pinpoint' (Levi 2014). We may assume that he is referring to the Chinese population: as far as the Portuguese are concerned, historians have become frustrated by the lack of Portuguese documentation, though it may be the case that records did exist but were lost, perhaps through fire or improper storage in humid conditions.

More is known, as Joseph Levi also points out, about the overall dining habits of the English/English-speaking populace of Macau, as recorded in the English literature. He is presumably referencing journals such as that by American Harriet Low Hilliard,[9] who lived in Macau with her aunt and uncle from 1829 to 1833, and who recounts elegant tiffin (a term for afternoon tea that emanated from British India) and grand Christmas dinners (Doling 1994, 9). She disliked taking tea in the Chinese manner without milk; and nor was congee (Chinese rice porridge) to her liking. She observes and notes down various points of culinary substitution. 'She had been making gingerbread, and not having any butter, the servant brought some mutton tallow, which she put in!'

It is also through this young American that we know about some of the more intimate aspects of the character and behaviours of British artist George Chinnery, who resided in Macau from 1825 until his death in 1852. He had moved to Madras in 1802 where he produced 'likenesses' of key British colonial figures, and on his arrival in Macau many sought his painterly skills. Yet alongside his portraiture he also sketched street life, and he returned many times to the food stalls outside São Domingo's Church. He was purportedly intelligent and entertaining company, but not at the dining table. Harriet Low Hilliard described him as 'a monstrous epicure' who was 'particularly disagreeable at breakfast, being something of a gourmand and not particular in his manner of eating'.

While we argue that there is little Chinese influence on Macanese cooking, the situation is rather more nuanced than might be expected. First, Macanese families have in other research from a decade or so ago reported that they eat Chinese and non-Macanese food several times a week—up to 70 per cent (Mamak 2007, 166). Did the Chinese-hired cooks of these families deliberately distinguish between Chinese and non-Chinese food; and did the Chinese deliberately avoid association of their cooking culture with Macanese? It is an interesting question, but almost certainly over time Macanese food began to incorporate more local ingredients such as Cantonese cuts of meat, which were familiar to the Chinese cook and easy to access on the street or at the wet market. We see this in dishes such as Tacho (Tacho means pot in Portuguese), also known as Chau Chau Pele, which seem to have almost entirely lost its Portuguese roots. A number of Macanese would refer to this winter casserole as their favourite, or among their favourite, Macanese dishes. Ingredients for Tacho include lap cheong (Chinese sausage), lap yuk (Chinese bacon), lap ap (smoked duck leg), as well as pig skin, pig trotter, and Chinese white cabbage.

It is likely that it was the influence of the hired Chinese cook that caused the Macanese to develop a parallel interest in food as medicine (an interest that was not prevalent among the Portuguese), as seen in dishes such as Chau Chau Parida; and to place food at the centre of culture in the broadest sense. This chicken and ginger dish was given to women as a tonic after child birth. It is also noteworthy that chau (to stir-fry, in Cantonese) is one of the few Cantonese/Chinese cooking terms to have been incorporated into the Macanese culinary canon.

The conundrum of the hired Chinese cook

Alexander Mamak makes an important point about the role of the cook. In the early evolution of Macanese cooking, the cook would have been a servant from another Portuguese colony, but once the Portuguese were comfortably settled in Macau they would begin to hire cooks and housekeepers locally. In contemporary Macau, these domestic helpers are mostly Filipino, but go back a few decades and they would almost certainly have been Chinese. He further argues that Portuguese cooking dominated early Macanese cooking, but infers that it perhaps later entered a phase of cultural diffusion, becoming integrated with the now more local cooking of the Cantonese (Mamak 2007, 163). When cuisines rub up alongside each other, and are prepared by cooks of varying nationalities, it is almost certain that they will borrow and share; that they will be eaten and consumed in reaction to changing manners and environments. Singapore provides an interesting case with, for example, the Islamisation of Chinese food. 'The three cuisines, ie Chinese, Malay and Indian, appropriate in a promiscuous and voracious manner from each other' (Chua and Rajah 2001, 164).

A level of similar 'promiscuous' activity in the context of Macau is visible in the following example. During the 1950s, Macanese snacks such as Chilicotes were available on the street, but this activity has not been attributed to Macau neighbourhoods but to downtown sections of Hong Kong. And such snacks were not being sold by the Macanese.

Chilicotes, deep-fried pastries, are traditionally stuffed with curried minced beef (perhaps mixed with minced pork) and finely chopped potato. To some extent they resemble dim sum crescents, but these are more likely steamed and fashioned out of rice rather than wheat flour. And they were being sold on the street not by Macanese but by Chinese men, known as the Merenda Men, who sensed a business opportunity in selling door to door the kinds of Macanese snacks that were so time-consuming to prepare at home. 'The Merenda Man could speak Macanese and knew how to cook some Macanese dishes although no one knows where he learned those skills' (Mamak 2007, 166). It is probable that the 'he' mentioned here learnt from his wife, who had previously worked for a Macanese family; and this idea is confirmed by Ivo Guterres, who has shared with me some fascinating insights into this cooking process and its results (personal correspondence, November 2017).

'Another aspect to be clarified is the relationship between the cook amahs and the Macanese ladies in their homes.[10] The amahs would have learnt the traditional Macanese cuisine directly from their supervisors (the Macanese ladies) and would have been very good in Macanese Cuisine by the end of each period with their land-ladies.' Perhaps feeling threatened by this skill based, Guterres believes that 'some ladies tried to disguise their recipes by taking some of the egg shells out from the garbage, etc. I do not think this was successful, the amahs would have known the number of eggs available or even such other condiments needed for a special dish.'

He had personal experience of the 'merenda', as he explains. 'The Macanese have the tendency of passing on [to] their cooks to others in the family of friends when they decide to change cooks or when these resigned or even when they migrated (this was our own case). From my own past memory of my times in Hong Kong (I was born in Hong Kong but left for Portugal and only returned in 1961 to 1971), I remember some of these amah cooks would then carry on as their own bosses and even gone back to their old Macanese connections (homes) with their wares with what is termed as "merenda" which they would come to sell on weekends. They would sell chilicotes, apa-bico, and all sorts of wonderful "petiscos" in baskets; probably they would have improved these to the point that everyone would be hoping they would come around to their homes each weekend. Their knowledge could have been passed down to their own families and for the benefit of their own enterprises.'

But the Merenda Man—or his wife, or more likely the pair of them together— might also have taken, say, the Chilicotes recipe in a different direction, substituting white radish for the potato, and then steaming it rather than frying it. For example, a recipe for Chilicotes, where they are steamed in banana leaf and stuffed with minced pork and Chinese preserved cabbage, appears alongside the traditional fried version in *Macanese Cooking: A Journey across Generations* (Jorge 2004, 50). As mentioned elsewhere in this research, Macanese dishes—with a Cantonese twist—are becoming increasingly available in Cantonese-Chinese restaurants in Macau, but the interest in, or ability of, Chinese to cook Macanese food is clearly no new phenomenon. At least not on the street.

In addition, Cantonese dishes have historically been served alongside Macanese dishes. Macanese cuisine does not feature much of a range of vegetable dishes, with the exception of South East Asian-style creations such as bitter gourd cooked in coconut milk, and eggplant sambal—both bitter gourd and eggplant being widely available in local markets, because they are very popular with the Cantonese. Most Macanese cooks (or cooks in Macanese families) would have cooked Cantonese-style vegetable dishes at home, such as stir-fried pak choi or choi sum, or steamed dau miu (pea shoots); or served a simple Portuguese-inspired salad of local lettuce, tomato, onion, and green bell pepper, studded with brined olives. Tony da Silva recalls his wider family growing tomatoes, peas, beans, and various green vegetables in their kitchen gardens in Macau (personal correspondence, January 2018), and it would be interesting to know in which ways these would have been prepared.

Macanese cuisine: (Ever) in transition

None of what is written in these pages should suggest that Macanese was a cuisine created 'just like that' in the earliest days of the Portuguese settlers in Macau, and that it stays confined to the philosophy of the original domestic kitchens of its birth. There is everything to suggest that it has always been a dynamic arena, reacting to multiple culinary conversations. Let's take a generic dish such as rice and beans (available in Macau in various forms) as a concrete example of how such conversations might play out, and how a single dish has highly significant but highly variable cultural meanings attributed to it across different cultures. In the publication *Rice and Beans: A Unique Dish in a Hundred Places* (Wilk and Barbosa, 2012) a series of contributions are made by writers showing how these two humble ingredients are combined into a single dish in so many different cultures. 'The Brazilian case is a good example of this,' we read in the introduction, and the two editors continue to explore the historical and economic trajectories of this pair of staples. 'Today rice and beans in Brazil are the embodiment of different values, ranging from the Brazilian myth of origin of being a racial democracy, to the expression of "Brazilian-ness" when away from home, the essence of family food, and the values of a mestizo nation' (Wilk and Barbosa 2012, 1).

The 'racial democracy' here referred to is assumed to refer to one account that the dish was created by President/Dictator Getulio Vargus, who presided from 1930 to 1945, as a unifying project. Beans (black), rice (white), pork (pink), and so on were culinarily joined in an attempt to do the almost impossible job of bringing some kind of democracy to a country with a long and complicated history, including colonialism and the slave trade, and a significant number of immigrants from countries as diverse as Germany and Japan.

A closer focus can specifically identity Feijoada, a dish we usually expect to be based on rice and beans, with the addition of various cuts of pork. From Brazil to Timor, everywhere the Portuguese went, a new version appeared. But is the dish originally Portuguese? It is widely viewed to be Brazilian in origin, created perhaps in the slave quarters of Bahia (Hamilton 2008, 102), in the north-eastern part of the country on the Atlantic coast. The story goes that slaves were given rations of rice and beans. They augmented these rations with cuts of pork thrown away by their masters—off-cuts such as ears and trotters—because the masters only wanted to eat the loin, the belly, the neck, and so on. However, the Portuguese are noted for their enthusiasm for tripe; and indeed there's a regional dish akin to Feijoada from Portugal's Tras-os-Montes region, in the mountainous north-east of the country, which is prepared with pig's ear, snout, and trotters, along with sausage, ham, and salt pork (Hamilton 2008, 102).

Again with a Brazil link, the Macanese shrimp and okra curry served at APOMAC club/restaurant in Macau is almost certainly from the Bahia region of Brazil, with okra having been introduced to Brazil by way of Mozambique. Okra is believed to have originated in East Africa, in Ethiopia, and it should be noted that okra is not generally grown or used in southern China, though it is common in Indian cooking. Soup noodle dish Lacassa is almost certainly a Macanese version, both linguistically and gustatorily, of the Laksa from Malacca; and pork organ dish Sarapatel is almost certainly based on Goan Sorpotel.

Other dishes are argued to be unique to Macau and the cooking of the Macanese, though this idea raises the question of whether any dish, in any cuisine, emerges without some memory of, or inspiration or borrowing from, another cuisine.

One of the Macanese repertoire's most iconic dishes is African Chicken, and it is here used, together with the quotidian Minchi, to garner some 'thick description' (after Clifford Geertz) as to what the complexities of Macanese cuisine are.[11] Its complexities are even reflected in the names of these dishes that might represent a number of linguistic influences—including the real, the imagined, and the defunct.

African Chicken

> 'Sadly with age the memory can play tricks on the taste buds. One example is the search for Angelo's African Chicken. Within our community around the world, there are legions of amateur cooks experimenting with various ingredients to replicate this famous dish. Funnily, with the passage of time, if we were presented today with a chicken cooked by Angelo himself, we might not recognise it.' —Ed Rozario, Melbourne, Australia (personal correspondence, 2012)

This dish likely dates to the 1940s, so it came late in the canon, and is also unusual for having been attributed to a bona fide chef rather than a home cook. It is thought to have been created by chef America Angelo (he died in 1979) at the former Pousada de Macau. However, there's an almost identical dish from Goa, where lime juice is included in the marinade and the chicken is deep fried (Fernandes 1990, 19). Macanese African Chicken also bears a resemblance to India's Butter Chicken, another restaurant favourite alongside Vindaloo. It is also known as Galinha a Cafreal, perhaps because of its final, rather blackened appearance: African slaves who worked on the ships were known as *cafres* (Jorge 2004: 82). Culinary links with Africa seem likely, perhaps following a visit by Angelo to one of Portugal's African colonies (probably Angola or Mozambique) by Angelo. It has also been noted that soldiers from Mozambique had sometimes been stationed in Macau, and it is possible that it is they who had introduced, or at least influenced, the dish. The recipe attributed to Chef Angelo involves a marinade of butter, garlic, chillies, coconut milk, and bay leaves; while versions available in Macau today are almost always made with a peanut and tomato-based sauce. Many chefs cooking the dish in contemporary Macau maximise the amount of sauce, which is then mopped up with bread.

Other interpretations and reproductions have emerged. In Abraham Conlon and Adrienne Lo's 2016 *The Adventures of Fat Rice: Recipes from the Chicago Restaurant inspired Inspired by Macau*, the recipe for African Chicken demonstrates the continuing reproduction and reinterpretation of the dish, this time far away in Chicago. They name the dish Galinha a Africana and come up with a combination of ingredients which that specifically recall the activities of the Portuguese in Asia. Juxtaposed are the sambals of Malacca, coriander of India, cinnamon of Ceylon (now Sri Lanka), fish sauce of Thailand, and the peanuts introduced across Asia during the Columbian Exchange, which occur so frequently in dipping sauces such as satay. Their marinade for the chicken includes Sichuan pepper, cayenne pepper, and piri piri; and the sauce in which the chicken is served sees the addition of freshly minced ginger; and spices such as cinnamon, ground coriander, and sweet paprika.

The recipe that follows was shared with this author by Tony da Silva, and is a 'pared back' version often believed to be very close to the original.

Galinha a Cafreal (African Chicken)

This recipe first appeared in Taste of Macau: Portuguese Cuisine on the China Coast *(Jackson 2003).*

1 small chicken (approx 1 kg)
75 g butter, softened
12 cloves garlic, finely chopped
1 tsp salt
2 bay leaves, crushed

4 small chillies, chopped
1 × 165 ml can coconut milk
1 tsp cornflour (optional)
1 tbsp chicken stock (optional)

Using a sharp knife, cut through the backbone of the chicken lengthways. Score the breastbone lengthways until you can press the chicken flat on a plate.

To prepare the marinade, mix 50 g butter, 8 cloves of chopped garlic, salt, bay leaves, and chillies into a paste. Spread paste over the chicken, cover, and leave to marinate overnight in the refrigerator.

To make the basting sauce, combine the remaining butter with the other 4 cloves of chopped garlic, add the coconut milk and stir well.

Place the chicken in a roasting tin and set under the over grill for about 1 hour. Baste regularly with the coconut milk mixture. When ready, the chicken should be blackened on top but still soft underneath. Before serving, stir sauce thoroughly and, if necessary, thicken with cornflour dissolved in a little chicken stock.

(Everyone Loves) Minchi

Minchi is often mentioned in poetry and other writing. There is a certain sense of solidarity and kinship when we speak about our taste for **minchi**, and a nostalgic wistfulness brings us together in our common 'culinary memory'—a special **minchi**, like this **minchi mosca**, made by someone who devotedly and deliciously brought joy to more than one generation at some time in the past, and whom nobody has yet equalled. Yes, because it's a high benchmark and the terms of comparison will always be in our taste buds... remembering Macau. (Jorge 2004, 104)

Macau novelist and lawyer Henrique de Senna Fernandes (1923–2010) remarked with much pride and nostalgia that not a day had gone by when he had not eaten Minchi (personal conversation, 1994), and it is dish significant enough to appear in Macanese literature. There are many different versions, but it is always served with steamed rice and (apparently more recently) with a flipped over fried egg on top. It is usually made with a combination of ground beef and ground pork (preferably cut by hand with two choppers) cooked in Portuguese olive oil, with the addition of diced onions and tiny cubes of fried potato; and a sauce composed of dark soy, light soy (and possibly kecap manis, the sweet soy sauce of Indonesian derivation), and Lea & Perrins Worcestershire Sauce—which was patented and first sold in the United Kingdom in 1837 (Mintz 2007, 203).

The inclusion of this sauce in the Minchi gravy suggests the dish may have been created following the arrival of the British in Hong Kong in 1841, this being an iconic

British seasoning that originated in colonial India before going into commercial production in the UK. The creation of this dish is indicative of a more than functioning relationship between the British and the Macanese. In addition to Cantonese and Portuguese, and the Macanese patuá,[12] the Macanese were able to speak English. It has even been suggested that the dish was created not in Macau but among the Macanese community in Hong Kong (Mamak 2007, 165).

This suggestion nuances the idea of the breadth of Macanese foodways. It may not refer to a dish created in Macau, but one created by a Macanese person. Indeed, Alexander Mamak has even posited that what constitutes a Macanese dish may be simply defined as one that is cooked by a person identifying as Macanese. 'There is only one reason why such dishes are called Macanese rather than Portuguese or Chinese, and that is because the Macanese people, and not anyone else, created them' (Mamak 2007, 167).

The term 'minchi' is thought to be a corruption of the English word 'mince' (Jackson 2003, 79) or 'to mince'. Other theories suggest that Minchi could be based on the Indian ground lamb dish Keema, which the Portuguese could have been exposed to (see, for example, Jorge 2004, 102); and indeed there is a recipe for Goan Masala Keema based not on lamb but a typical ingredient of Minchi, ground beef.[13]

Henrique de Senna Fernandes has commented that everyone likes their Minchi this way or that, implying that there is no one definitive way of cooking it, and within his own family he said that a variety of Minchi dishes would be served at a single lunch or dinner (personal conversation, 1994). However, the dish has further mutated in Macanese kitchens from being ground/finely chopped pork and/or beef-based to something possibly based on shrimp, or including cloud-ear mushrooms, preserved salted vegetables, bitter gourd, what is often called turnip but is in fact radish/kolrabi, and a topping of crispy fried rice vermicelli (see, for example, Jorge 2004, 100–104; and Mamak 2007, 165). Such variations indicate a gradual evolution towards the inclusion of local ingredients more typical of local Cantonese dishes. Such indicates the creativity of the Chinese domestic cook to start with and, later, is indicative of the intermarrying of Macanese with Cantonese and the resultant cultural diffusion.

Minchi (Mince, with Soy Sauce)

This recipe first appeared in Taste of Macau: Portuguese Cuisine on the China Coast *(Jackson 2003).*

500 g mixed minced pork and beef
2 medium potatoes
olive oil for frying
1 onion, finely chopped
1 bay leaf
1 clove garlic, smashed

salt and pepper to taste
3 tbsp light soy sauce
pinch sugar
1 tsp Worcestershire sauce

Dice potatoes into 1 cm cubes and fry in olive oil until golden brown. Drain and set aside.

Heat a little olive oil in another pan, add onion and bay leaf, sauté until onion is soft and golden. Set aside.

Add crushed garlic and a teaspoon of olive oil in the same pan, and continue to heat. Press garlic and circulate it around the pan to free the aroma. Discard garlic once it is golden brown.

Increase heat to high, add minced meat to the pan with a pinch of salt, and press constantly to break meat down.

Cook for about 4 minutes and when the minced meat is nearly broken up add reserved onion and bay leaf. Test for seasoning and add salt and pepper. Stir for 2 minutes.

Combine soy sauce, sugar, and Worcestershire sauce, and pour this mixture on to the meat. Stir well for 3–5 minutes until the minced meat is broken up and the mixture is becoming dry.

Add potatoes, mix well, and serve.

Macanese cooking and globalisation

Veteran Macanese cook Aida Jesus still oversees the daily running of Riquexo, but both here and at APOMAC, a club for Macanese but with a restaurant open to the public, young Filipinos have been taught how to prepare Macanese dishes. Principally Portuguese restaurants such as A Lorcha and Litoral serve Macanese dishes, as does the Educational Restaurant at Macau's Institute of Tourism Studies (IFT).

There's the risk, though, that Macanese cuisine will be reduced to a repertoire of just a handful of dishes, all adapted to suit the hotel guest. Perhaps adaptation is not quite the threat it might be seen as: the nature of Macanese food is adaptation, as is particularly true for domestic kitchen-based cuisines. Some dishes probably never made it past the first post or remained the domain of just one family. Lard would be seen as an essential part of the flavour and texture of Arroz Carregado, a firmly textured pressed rice dish pricked with spring onions and traditionally served with Porco Balichão Tamarinho. Yet cooking with lard has ceased to be popular (or essential, in terms of using every single last piece of the pig) and has been replaced by butter, or elsewhere with olive oil, altering flavours and texture in the recreation of a typical dish.

Figure 5.10: Aida Jesus, circa 2015.
Photo courtesy of Sonia Palmer.

Musing on the Macanese concoction Po Kok Gai (Portuguese Chicken Curry), Abraham Conlon addresses the decoration of this dish, which might include hard-boiled egg, olives, and chouriço. '[They were] likely added much later,' he writes, 'by clever twentieth-century restaurateurs who either wanted to make the dish more "exotic" for Chinese tourists or more "Portuguese" for visiting Portuguese dignitaries' (Conlon and Lo 2016, 181).

Balichão: A Unique-ish Preparation in Macau

Balichão, a fermented fish sauce made with krill, is not used in every dish, but it is a condiment unique to Macanese cuisine. It is almost certainly inspired by the Belacan of Malaysia and Indonesia (see Chapter 4 for further explanation) and the Cincaluk of Malacca (also see Chapter 4); but the Greek-Roman fish sauce of Garum had already graced European dining tables (though there was also a 'poor man's' version). Krill are tiny, translucent shrimps that used to be found in abundance in the upper reaches of the Pearl River Delta, but which are now difficult to acquire. They are combined with Portuguese brandy or wine, chilli, lemon, peppercorns, and bay leaf, and then left in a clay urn for three months or so. Almost no one today is making it in this traditional way, instead substituting Belacan as the base ingredient, and perhaps mixing it with the other component parts such as bay leaf—though the resultant taste is quite different. This sauce is used as a component part of dishes—it is not a dipping sauce—and it is fried before use. Like all fish or seafood preparations, fermented or otherwise, it is highly pungent, and a good source of nutrition, as well as flavour. It forms a particularly central role in the Malay-inspired dish Porco Balichão Tamarinho, where it adds an extra layer of flavour, and in noodle soup dish Lacassa, where it heightens aromas, together with sprigs of fresh coriander leaves. Balichão is almost certainly the precursor of the Cantonese salted shrimp paste, haam-ha-cheung, showing how Macanese cuisine would in turn have some influence on another local/Chinese culinary culture.

Desserts, or perhaps not desserts as this word suggests consumption after a savoury meal, is another obvious area where Macanese sweets have influenced local fare. They have been, in turn, influenced by Portuguese sweet-stuffs from different starting places in Asia. We refer here to the soupy concoctions made variously with coconut, sago, tapioca, mango, yam, beans, and jaggery, all of which concoctions used to be widely available to buy in Macau.

> ### Balichão
>
> *This recipe first appeared in* Taste of Macau: Portuguese Cuisine on the China Coast *(Jackson 2003)*
>
> This recipe was offered by Isabel Eusebio, owner of the former Macau restaurant called Balichão. The cate (approx. 500 g) and the tael (approx. 30 g) are the traditional measurements of wet markets in Guangdong Province, including those in Macau and Hong Kong.
>
> 10 cate shrimp
> 3 cate salt
> 8 tael Shaoxing (a Chinese cooking wine akin to sherry)
> 4 tael Portuguese brandy
> 2 tael peppercorns
> 1 tael bay leaves, crushed
> 3 lemons, juiced and cut into quarters
> 1–2 tael chillies
>
> Mix together, seal jar, and leave for 3 months!

Conclusion

The breadth of the Macanese cannon attests to the breadth of the ethnicities mixed together and represented in the community, and Macanese people can be deemed to have sophisticated palates that appreciate a broad range of flavours, textures, and sensations. Flavour combinations were born here that would have been unfamiliar to Asian and European palates alike. Dishes range from subtle noodle soup or deep-fried vegetarian pastries through to rich meat stews and spicy seafood curries, and sweet snacks, cakes, and desserts. Macanese cuisine has also absorbed Portuguese dishes to the point that they would be considered Macanese, particularly salt-cod dishes such as Pastéis de Bacalhau.

The food moniker of 'fusion' has done little to progress the study of the organic nature of cuisine. Macanese cooking has sometimes been labelled the world's first fusion cooking, and there might be some truth here, in the sense that it juxtaposed ingredients that had likely never shared space: soy sauce and rosemary, for example.

But fusion implies that you're fusing something concrete to something concrete, which is not the case here. Portuguese foodways may have originally been the foundations of Macanese foodways—though represented in a third space, many miles from the motherland—but here we have the cooking styles, ingredients, and traditions of multiple cultures coming together to create something entirely new. This process is distinct from hybridity, which refers to a process that results in the changing of culinary traditions and habits within a single culture. Fusion food, as represented in the public domain, is an entirely conscious creative act of (re)production, something performed. Are these distinctions important within culinary discourse? Certainly they can help us to explore foodways that go far beyond the linear and geographical delimitations we have tended to assume.

Conclusion

> My chutneys and kassundies are, after all, connected to my nocturnal scribblings—by day, amongst the pickle vats, by night within these sheets, I spend my time at the great work of preserving. Memory, as well as fruit, is being saved from the corruption of the clocks.
> —Salman Rushdie, *Midnight's Children*

Barely mid-morning, under a streaming sun and, close to the city's tram line, long queues have already formed outside a café in Lisboa, famous for the Portuguese pastry, pastéis de nata. Here we are in the shadows of the Jerónimus Monastery in the district of Belém, at Pastéis de Belém.[1] The venue was purportedly established in 1837—and it is here and then that the famous egg tart, surely Portugal's most famous culinary export, was born; known here not as pastéis de nata but rather grandly as pastéis de Belém. This sweet, creamy, and eggy pastry tart was said to be created by a monk from the monastery—from whence so many Portuguese desserts and sweetmeats emanated—seeking to make a living. Its popularity spread.

The daily thousandfold sprinkling of ground cinnamon on the top of each pastel de nata has reached such quotidian proportions that it might be forgotten that cinnamon is not a part of traditional Portuguese cooking mores.[2] It is not cultivated in Portugal. Rather, it was introduced, from Sri Lanka (then referred to by colonial powers as Ceylon) via the spice trade, in which Portugal played an important part, and was embraced, along with other spices such as nutmeg and clove, by European cooks. Spices, costly and exotic, were used as markers of wealth and prestige, incorporated

Figure 6.1: Pastel de nata.

perhaps with flaked almonds in a Venetian risotto; or alongside dried fruit in an English pulled pie of chopped beef with carrot. Warm spices were then part of the savoury canon, utilised not only in the sweet sections of the pastry kitchen.

Culinary narratives among colonising nations have traditionally assessed the culinary influences of, broadly speaking, the coloniser on the colonised. The Vindaloo of Goa, for example, was of direct Portuguese genesis, and comprised a European (marinating) technique interacting with local produce, including spices. Secondary narratives have concerned themselves with the acculturation of a dish. The British found the Indian kebab of egg cased in spicy ground mutton appealing, but felt they were profoundly improving upon it by replacing mutton with pork and the spices with green herbs such as sage from the kitchen garden.

Yet as the example of a sprinkle of cinnamon shows, influences have gone in multiple directions. The spice mix Vadouvan—usually comprising cumin seeds, mustard seeds, and fenugreek with shallots and garlic—is a French derivation of an Indian masala from Puducherry. The iconic Lea & Perrins Worcestershire Sauce represented the commercialisation by two chemists in 1830s England of a condiment discovered in Bengal by a lord. Loaded onto British ships due for the colonies, it went on to become a component part of both Kristang and Macanese cooking.

People, Produce, and Practice

In any study concerning the Portuguese of culinary practices—and indeed agricultural practices—it is necessary to go back yet further to the Columbian Exchange, and thereafter to the spice trade. These two massive global movements represented extraordinary global communication that would change exactly what was grown where, and subsequently what was cooked where.

The spice trade opened up global economic relations and illuminated existing cross-cultural exchanges and affiliations being enacted along the Spice Route. In addition, as alluded to above, it changed European cooking habits, at least for those who occupied the elite stratifications. The effects of the Columbian Exchange, delivered by the Portuguese (and the Spanish) were perhaps more profound in that they transformed not only agricultural practice and introduced new agricultural products, but they also transformed diets—and life expectancy. The humble chilli pepper, for example, delivered high levels of Vitamin C, a vital nutrient, but could also bring life to a humble bowl of steamed rice, topped perhaps with a sliver of chicken or some torn leafy greens. Alternative starch sources such as potatoes and sweet potato also became available.

To follow this introduction of new produce were processes, in the hands of the Portuguese, of entirely new ways to prepare such produce and cook such produce. Culinary conversations were already taking place in Goa, notably in the creation of the world's most famous 'curry': Vindaloo. The term has nothing to do with the Indian term for potato—aloo—but is rather a corruption and conflation of two Portuguese words, *vinho* (wine) and *alho* (garlic). This dish reflects a tradition on the island of Madeira to marinade pork in wine (or vinegar; or, in the case of Goa, coconut vinegar), and this cooking technique was introduced to India. All pork-based dishes in Goa are of Portuguese origin. Next, the Portuguese established a trading base in Malacca, much closer geographically to Macau. Here, their colonial strategy continued to involve marrying into local families, the descendants of these families becoming known as a mixed-race community called the Kristang. From these 'hybrid' kitchens emerged specific cooking styles and flavours, and many of these dishes have much in common with the cooking of the Macanese, as well as with Malay cooking.

What Is Macanese Cuisine?

The colonial situation was to be different when the Portuguese arrived in Macau, on the Pearl River Delta, and this tiny territory became a semi-official part of Portugal's Asian empire. There was no indigenous population—just a few fishing families who lived on their boats—thus no women to convert to Christianity and then marry. Significantly, then, there was no Chinese 'culture' as such and certainly no indigenous cuisine. There might not be, then, any local Chinese influences on the resultant Macanese cuisine.

The Portuguese, faced with these new conditions, brought along wives and servants from Goa, from Malacca, and from countries such as Japan and the Philippines with which they were enjoying trading relations. These women brought with them intangible cultural skills, and knowledge of a variety of Asian cuisines and ingredients that were not native to southern China. Spices with which they were familiar—cinnamon, cloves, coriander seeds, nutmeg—were available in Macau because of the spice trade, via the Portuguese ships.

Further, the Pearl River Delta was, or had become partly thanks to the Columbian Exchange, agriculturally rich. The stapes of the Portuguese diet, then, on which Macanese cuisine would centre—fish and seafood, pork and chicken; potatoes and onions; and eggs—were all in plentiful supply. To a Portuguese dish of fried chicken were added coconut milk and chilli. Pork and onion stew went in a completely different direction with the richness of belachan and the sweetness of jaggery. Ginger and cumin ameliorated the aromas of tripe; and steamed shrimp was elevated with papaya flowers and chopped red chilli. The emergence of a subsequent Macanese cuisine can be traced back through a variety of strands, including personal and family; sense of community; and indeed a sense of competitiveness within that community as to who could best prepare, say, curried crab.

And, thus, a unique cuisine was born. Or was it—unique?

Intra-Asia Culinary Conversations

It has perhaps been assumed, given that the Portuguese settled first in Goa, thereafter in Malacca, and only after that in Macau, that any culinary conversations that may

Conclusion

have come about would have started in Goa, subsequently moved to Malacca by way of culinary influence, and thereafter from Malacca into Macau.

To start with, implicit here is the assumption that there was such a thing as a Goan 'cuisine', when in fact it had already encountered Arab influence, for example. In the same way, the suggestion of a distinctive Malaysian foodway is upset by the forces of conquerors and colonialism; and in Peranakan cooking we might see foodways that need to be defined within the cultural domain and quite beyond ethnicity. In other words, a dish deemed to be Chinese could have been appropriated by another community based not on the recipe, but on assumed meaning and use of that dish. If we can see that Macanese cuisine was influenced by the cooking of Malacca, it is no longer possible to argue that there was no Chinese influence on the cuisine, even if it may be possible to say that this influence did not come from the China territory of Macau, but via Chinese immigrants to Malacca and its environs.

The intra-Asia Peranakan community was already well established prior to the arrival of the Portuguese, and this community had created a cuisine that existed outside and beyond the indigenous Malay cuisine. Early Chinese immigrants are assumed to have found that the local dishes did not suit their taste buds, but the ingredients with which they were familiar were unavailable. Thus, they began to reproduce their own cooking by substituting foodstuffs which were available locally.

What is termed Peranakan culture, or Nyonya-Baba, is generally defined in terms of the settling and marrying of Chinese immigrants from the early fifteenth century with local women. It is quite possible that the rules of Islam were then not too strict, and Malaysian women could be acquired as wives and concubines by foreigners (non-Muslims). It is also possible that, for example, baby girl Malaysian orphans were raised by Chinese, and thus became culturally available for marriage among Chinese. However, it has been argued that the Baba are a product of influences that transcend both Chinese and Malay cultures.

So it was into this already vibrant intra-Asian culinary conversation that the Portuguese were introduced. In the process of their marrying into the local community—Christians who may have been of Malay or Chinese descent, or both—they came into contact with a hybrid cuisine. Fermented fish paste—belachan, geographically of both Indonesian and Malaysian extraction—would go on to frame the Portuguese-influenced cooking in the domestic kitchen, as would sophisticated spice mixes (rempah).

The cooking of Portuguese descendants, the so-called Kristang community in Malacca—with their mixed Portuguese and Asian ancestry, in a sense a community reflective of the Macanese people themselves—informs many aspects of Macanese cuisine. Let's take the Macanese dish Porco Balichão Tamarinho, very much influenced by Malay cooking traditions, and the Kristang Kari Porku Tambrinhyu, as one example. The core ingredients—pork, shrimp paste, tamarind—are almost identical, the difference being the addition by the Kristang of Malaysian rempah (spices). As another example, Kristang Debal and Macanese Diabo are both served at Christmas and both take the name of 'Devil'. While the 'recipes' may not look too similar at a cursory glance, both incorporate the strong and distinctive flavours of vinegar and mustard. As an aside, there are also British influences on both Kristang cuisine and Macanese cuisine in the British period in Malaysia and after the cessation of Hong Kong to the British, respectively.

Yet at the same time as these similarities have been noted, there's evidence that the descendants of the Portuguese in Goa were also cooking similar dishes. There are many examples of dishes that we would consider to be central to the Macanese canon that also appear in cookbooks from Goa, such as Sorpotel, Sarabulho, Galinha Cafreal, and Feijoada (*sic*). It has also been suggested that the Portuguese brought Chinese culinary traditions to Goa from Malacca and Macau. How was such a culinary exchange orchestrated? It is possible that the Church played an important role.

As a result of the Church's outreach, Christians were also emerging from, for example, trading partner Japan. These young men, training for the priesthood, were moving across oceans between Malacca, Goa, Macau, and Portugal. Culinary conversations were almost certainly happening during these tedious and treacherous voyages. These could have been occurring among the culturally and ethnically diverse crew members and with a ship's cooks, as well as with those passengers for whom they prepared the food. Such interactions are highly suggestive of the fact that culinary conversations were not occurring in a single direction, in an Occidental-Oriental binary; and nor they did not happen chronologically in colonial acquisition terms.

There were quite likely Cantonese influences on Macanese cuisine into the twentieth century, or at least adaptations. We have the interesting anomaly of the so-called Merenda Man; the man who sold Macanese snack foods such as Chilicotes to the Macanese community in Hong Kong. It is assumed that the wives of these entrepreneurs had previously worked in Macanese households, and subsequently shared recipes with their husbands. Over time these snacks could become more 'Cantonese' in terms of using cheap local ingredients with which to stuff these little pastries, or even enclosing them in rice flour wrappers, rather than baking them in a wheat-flour based pastry. As an aside, it should be noted that most Cantonese dim sum are steamed, though some have a wheat flour pastry casing and are baked.

Finally, intra-Asian conversations can be defined within the context of a most important single condiment. The fermented fish paste belachan, generally purchased in block or sliced form, is associated with the territories which that we would now call Indonesia and Malaysia. During the Portuguese period in Malacca, a new fermented shrimp sauce was created, known as cincaluk. It seems that the Macanese Balichão is in turn a kind of version of cincaluk; and Balichão also appears in Goa under very similar names: Ballchow or Balchao. In a quite surprising move, Balichão is believed, via Macau, to have been the inspiration for the Cantonese fermented fish condiment [*yulu* 魚露]; and all the while recalling garum, the fish sauce of the Romans, as noted by Pliny the Elder, in *Natural History*, as 'the liquor from putrefaction'.

Macanese Cuisine: Its Perception

So is Macanese actually a unique cuisine, created in Macau, centring on Portuguese staples and locally growing produce, but accented with Asian flavours and Asian sensibilities? An anchor of this book has been to explore the emergence of a unique cuisine created in Macau by the colonial Portuguese and their households.

But why would we now be asking global and contemporary questions about a cuisine created some 450 years ago in a tiny part of China?

Macanese cuisine was perceived to be in danger of dying out in Macau, and a question had to be asked about its fate in the continuing face of diaspora. Additionally, what transformative processes have been taking place against the backdrop of a transforming Macau, emerging from its image as Hong Kong's country cousin to a glitzy gambling destination that is even overtaking Las Vegas in terms of gaming revenues. A survey was thus conducted to explore how Macanese in the diaspora felt about Macanese food, with particular reference to the preservation or otherwise of the cuisine.

A Sense of Place: Macau

> Two weeks in his homeland after an absence of twenty-four years had hardly been enough. It would have been better if he hadn't come back. But how could a Macanese turn down the chance of seeing his homeland again . . . He had made full use of his stay. He had satisfied his long craving for Macanese and Chinese food, savoured with their own local ingredients.
>
> —Henrique de Senna Fernandes, 'Candy'

The SurveyMonkey carried out in 2017 among the Macanese diaspora was partly conceived in response to the fact that there are more Macanese living outside Macau than within. Estimates of how many Macanese live in Macau are no more than guesswork: anecdotal figures mooted in the community vary widely from 3,500 to between 10,000 and 20,000. The Macau population stands at 650,000, with women outnumbering men, but there are no official census figures dividing the population by ethnicity/nationality. It should also be noted that the Portuguese community has probably never numbered above 7,000.

As background, Macanese cuisine only started to become visible in Macau from the late 1980s, when a number of independent Macanese restaurants began to emerge. The first ever Macanese restaurant was Riquexo, which opened in 1978. From the 2000s, Macanese cookbooks began to be published. Macanese cooking was seeing its transformation from something humble, produced in the domestic kitchen, to something that was listed on the menus of restaurants in five-star casino hotels. Macanese food was becoming part of the cultural tourism package. Indeed, government initiatives that are in place require new hotels to offer Portuguese and Macanese food, as well as Portuguese wine. Further, small independent businesses receive a tax break when they do likewise.

The new-found visibility of Macanese food has not come without a cost. There is much culinary confusion around what exactly constitutes Macanese food and what constitutes Portuguese food, or whether there might be any crossover.

One (non-casino) hotel restaurant lists twelve Portuguese and Macanese dishes on its menu, such as Arroz de Pato (Duck Rice) and Galinha Piri Piri, which is translated into English on the menu as African Chicken. Another menu features a 'local' Portuguese and Macanese page, with dishes including Fried Macanese Prawns, Bacalhau a Bras, and Caldo Verde. To briefly analyse the above listings, Galinha Piri Piri and African Chicken are in fact quite separate dishes, though both probably have African origins. Only Fried Macanese Prawns could be considered 'authentically' Macanese; while Duck Rice, Bacalhau a Bras, and Caldo Verde would be considered 'authentic' Portuguese.

Hospitality industry insiders, and indeed Macanese beyond, believe more effort should be made to help communicate the cuisines of Macau. It is certainly questionable as to whether tourists visiting Macau are able to name a Macanese dish.There are queues for pastéis de nata (egg tarts) at Lord Stow's in Coloane Village; for pork chop buns in the old Taipa village; and for gift boxes of almond cookies in various downtown locations. But the former is Portuguese (and in this case the 'secret' recipe is one created by a British pharmacist); and the latter two should technically be defined as 'Macau' food. Some elements of the tourist crowd might be able to name African Chicken, and indeed this is sometimes referred to as the national dish of Macau, but could they or would they place this within the Macanese canon; and indeed would they even know of the existence of distinct Macanese foodways? One mainland Chinese blogger expressed surprise when she was served a kind of curry with steamed rice in what she assumed to be a Portuguese restaurant.

Further, some point to the similarities between Macanese and Cantonese cooking, and many small Cantonese restaurants now offer local/Macanese specialities. Chinese chefs, even those trained in Macanese cooking, are likely to annotate recipes to suit either local palates or the tastes of tourists, mainland Chinese in particular. Such adaptations are regarded, among the Macanese, as a kind of culinary hijacking.

At the foundation of these culinary contestations are indications of the nature of the Macanese themselves, and how their identity has changed over time. At different points in history, Macanese-ness has been viewed as an absolute strength. At other points, the cultural capital of being of Portuguese descent has been emphasised; or of being more broadly of European descent. Being 'local', that is understanding local culture and being able to speak Cantonese (in addition to Portuguese and English), has also been stressed at certain times. Some families, with closer ties to Portugal, have tended to eat more Portuguese and Macanese food at home, while once Macanese marry into Cantonese families their eating habits are similarly affected. We also have the case of the Chinese cook, who would surely have cooked Cantonese food for her Macanese employer; and there is evidence that canny, entrepreneurial Cantonese—known as the

Merenda Men—began to cook Macanese snacks on the street for people who were too busy to make them at home.

Leaving Macau: The Diaspora

There is no single diaspora, and movement out of Macau has occurred for different reasons over time. Some left Macau for a better life, for education, for more opportunities; or during wartime and economic hardship; and in particular prior to Handover in December 1999. At this historic juncture, there was significant anxiety about China taking Macau away from the Macanese who feel themselves to be the indigenous people of Macau.

Neither is there a single diaspora in terms of the relationship maintained with Macau, the motherland. There is a significant and strong Macanese community in Hong Kong, which is just one hour from Macau by ferry, but few in this community visit Macau often or have much of a relationship with it. On the other hand, Macanese who have relocated to Canada, to Australia, to the USA, reveal very strong bonds with Macau.

The food anthropologist considers the nature of that bond in terms of Macanese food, which presents as one of the few cultural identifiers remaining within the community, or perhaps the only one. Research for this book began as a research paper entitled 'Memory and Identity: Macanese Cuisine in the Diaspora', with research including a global survey (hosted by SurveyMonkey) disseminated through the Casa movement.

There is little question of how important this movement, together with various other Macanese associations, has been for the preservation and celebration of Macanese culture in the diaspora, and through the regular conferences held in Macau for members of these Casas. One survey respondent even commented that he joined a Casa to pay tribute to, and to feel closer to, his (deceased) parents. The first Casa to be launched was Club Lusitano in Hong Kong, 150 years ago, followed by Club Recreio in 1906. Casa de Macau in Portugal was established in 1967; followed by the co-opting of various Casas and clubs in the USA, Canada, Australia, and Brazil. The most recent to be co-opted was the UK's Macau Home, in 2016. The Council of Macanese Communities (Conselho das Comunidades Macaenses, CCM) was founded in 2004 with a remit to manage all the Macanese associations, which now number nineteen. Of these, thirteen are in the diaspora and six in Macau.

Minchi: An icon

Based on survey results, it is notable how recipes and dishes, and remembrance of dishes, take some members of the Macanese diaspora powerfully back to the physical space of Macau. Some further stressed how their (loving, nostalgic) relationship with Macau should be seen as an important part of their cultural identity. Two respondents were both highly specific in the way that the iconic dish Minchi is not just a dish. In some way it becomes the embodiment of Macau.

The following comment related specifically to the recall of Minchi, on a return visit to Macau. 'You are walking along the streets you feel like that you belong there and since the long absence you feel like you were born again there.' Another wrote: 'Minchi is more than just a dish, it's a dish that in some way represents the Macanese . . . The mere mention of the word Minchi would indicate one's connection with Macau.' One respondent wrote that young Macanese without attachment to Macau love the food; and another said that all the younger members of his family at least loved Minchi.

In the end, then, the amelioration of loss may not even be about the Macanese cuisine as a whole, but only about a dish named Minchi, which itself was a later Macanese creation emanating from neighbouring Hong Kong (this is assumed based on the mixing of Lea & Perrins with soy sauce). Minchi . . . Minchi as the lone symbol, the last memory, the last flavour of Macanese food culture; Minchi as the dish reproduced in domestic kitchens from Lisboa to Melbourne, but simultaneously in an imaginary Macau, figuratively inhabited by the Macanese.

A Place for Cuisine; a Place for Recipes?

As has been explored in this book, reaching a consensus on what constitutes a cuisine is not always straightforward. Food anthropologist Sidney Mintz has argued that a cuisine is not a series of recipes printed in a cookbook or a series of dishes associated with a particular setting. Rather, he suggests that for a cuisine to come into being it needs to be eaten with sufficient frequency that those cooking and consuming it can be considered experts. These experts know how it is made, what is consists of, and, critically, care about such details. The key here is common social roots.

In the quest to ascertain the relative importance of Macanese cuisine in the formation of Macanese identity, suggested in the common social roots of Mintz, above, I asked two complementary questions in the survey. The first was to find out who prepares the Macanese food that is eaten; and the second was to discover how many people would rank it as their favourite food. There was a strong correlation between those who answered that they personally cooked Macanese food and the frequency of its consumption. Those who answered that it was prepared by someone Macanese from outside the family (quite likely someone at a Casa) only consumed Macanese food monthly, or annually.

As to the question of whether or not Macanese was your favourite cuisine, the geographical variation was quite striking. Of those respondents based in Macau, 75 per cent said it was their favourite, showing a direct correlation with the percentages of those eating Macanese food regularly and with their strong sense of identity around Macanese food. In the wider diaspora, just over 60 per cent said it was their favourite, which was slightly lower than the percentage who said Macanese food was an important part of their identity. In Hong Kong, the number who said it was their favourite was the lowest, at 57 per cent, though, in common with the greater diaspora, was slightly lower than those who expressed the importance of Macanese food in the context of their cultural identity rather than culinary preferences.

Macanese cuisine does not have to be your favourite, you may never cook it yourself, and you may eat it only rarely—but its importance is clearly embedded in Macanese identity. What is important is who cooks it (probably Mum), with whom it is eaten (family, community), and when it is eaten (at Christmas, at a christening, or at a wedding anniversary, for example). It is more than apparent that a cuisine, or a dish, may be favoured beyond all other, yet its literal consumption may only be once a year. Macanese cuisine is loved, is discussed, and is even embraced by younger Macanese people who show scant interest in their broader culture, or in the place called Macau, which they may never have visited. But there is evidence to suggest it is moving from being an everyday production of food in a domestic setting, *habitus* in the Bourdieu sense,[3] to something ritualised, ceremonial, symbolic, commodified; and even performed as a self-conscious act.[4]

Recipes: To share or not to share?

The loss of culinary culture is widely attributed to the process wherein knowledge is not being properly disseminated. Macanese cuisine has traditionally been passed as part of an oral tradition: learning with one's mother or grandmother in the kitchen through observation and practice. Associated with the Macanese community has been a traditional hostility towards sharing recipes, particularly the sharing of recipes beyond the family grouping.

Macanese subjects I interviewed in Macau in October 2017, in describing Macanese culinary culture, used terminology such as 'dying' and 'losing'; 'subsumed' and 'condemned'; and described Macanese food in the public arena in Macau sometimes in terms as strong as 'pseudo' and 'bastardised'. There's a tension, then, between, identity, meaning positive emotions in the Macanese community around Macanese cuisine, and how it is physically represented.

If there has been a traditional reluctance to share recipes, an important exception to this is the Macanese recipe Anthology, a product of a manual typewriter in Shanghai in the 1930s, which reached Hong Kong too. It is more than likely that this Anthology represented the first time that Macanese recipes had been recorded within the community, but outside the confines of the family, and subsequently entered the public domain. It marks a time when, because of the diaspora and the dissolution of the Macanese community in Macau, what was cooked at home by Macanese families began to inhabit a more public space as a marker of cultural identity; or Otherness. It has been argued that the defining of a cuisine becomes more important in certain cultural settings as it validates and authenticates a certain people.

So within the survey I raised questions regarding first the propensity to share recipes; and second about attitudes to cookbooks. The question of the sharing of

Macanese recipes also evoked strong emotion. Respondents used terms such as 'selfishness' and 'stupidity', or 'disappointed', to describe their attitude to those who have refused to share.

Indeed, Macanese food takes on importance at many levels beyond the spoon and fork. Man shall not live by bread alone? Macanese food goes far beyond calories, nutrients, and sustenance. This comment is instructive: 'I do my best to cook for my grandchildren at every opportunity *so that the tastes will be embedded in them from a young age*' (my emphasis); as is this one: 'Most of us of the Macanese diaspora *cling* to our heritage, like most migrants, via our traditional food' (my italics). The relationship of the Macanese, then, to Macanese food is profoundly complex; and further, occupies multiple spaces—the domestic setting, Macau the place, and within the global diaspora—and then assumes different meanings. 'Food provides a fluid symbolic medium for making statements about identity' (James 1997, 74).

A case for cookbooks

The reaction to questions about Macanese cookbooks yet again evoked strong emotion. One respondent suggested that given the publication of a number of Macanese cookbooks, the risk of loss of recipes and cooking traditions was not high—but he was very much a lone voice on this subject. There is scant enthusiasm, and certainly no praise for Macanese cookbooks, within the broader Macanese community. Perhaps even the reverse is true, based on comments garnered during this research.

Yet survey responses indicated that as many as two-thirds of those surveyed opened a Macanese cookbook at least occasionally—but clearly only rather apologetically, and even disparagingly. Respondents noted that they might refer to the 'one' Macanese cookbook they own; or that they refer to privately distributed informal 'cookbooks', and to records of family recipes preserved in the form of scrapbooks and the like.

This apparent disengagement with cookbooks, even as half of respondents use them regularly, certainly deserves some analysis. The respondent quoted above as seeing the value of cookbooks for recipe preservation, makes an additional comment, however, and I wonder if the key to the disparity lies here: 'Family specific variations are interesting but mostly will die with the family's last members.'

Even while recipes and tips are being shared within families, cookbooks might be perceived to be enhancing and even cementing the sense of loss of Macanese cuisine; or Macanese culture. In moving Macanese cooking away from a simple, everyday practice, and into the global culinary arena, there's almost a sense of alienation from published Macanese recipes. Recipes might deliver reasonably reliable lists of ingredients and even some technical hints—but they don't deliver Mother. The suggestion is that it is not enough to talk about the relationship between food and identity, for the actual recipe serves as a kind of conduit between the two and thus itself becomes an important part of identity, most particularly when it is a family recipe passed down. Based on survey findings, the importance of family, but most particularly the mother or the grandmother involved in the preparation of food, is central. Dishes and recipes are symbolic of family, and of Mother. It may only be the next generation/s who without any surviving aunt to call for an ingredient tip, will see cookbooks as perhaps something of cultural value. But that's for later research.

Critics argue that a culture—a language, a cuisine—exists only so long as it is useful. Macanese cooking endures, reconfigured again, but it may never have existed in a pure form. Rather, it has continually evolved, through a series of intra-Asia culinary conversations over 450 years. It has moved from domestic kitchen to hotel dining rooms; lost, perhaps, apart from the myriad meanings and memories of Minchi. Yet it has been simultaneously saved from the 'corruption of the clocks' by the chef in the casino.

Appendix 1
Background and Methodology

The Macanese diaspora is supported by the Council of Macanese Communities (Conselho das Comunidades Macaenses), on which the various Casas de Macau each have two representatives. This is a private, not-for-profit, non-government organisation established to, among other objectives, help join communities together, and disseminate reliable information about the history of Macau and the Macanese, particularly for the benefit of younger members of the diaspora.

There are Casas in Canada (Vancouver and Toronto), the USA (California), Australia (Sydney and Melbourne), Brazil (Sao Paulo and Rio de Janeiro), Portugal (Lisbon), the UK, and Hong Kong. It was through these Casas that the first tranche of (mainly quantitative) research was administered.

Conferences are held every few years in Macau, Econtro das Comunidades Macaenses (there is also one especially for younger people), which are partially Macau government funded, which bring together representatives of each Casa for meetings, cooking competitions, conferences, and so on. This author has spoken at a number of these conferences, thereby having the chance to meet Macanese from all over the world, and thus has contacts in many places.

Besides overseas Macanese already personally known to the author being selected for interview, informants were identified (sampling) by various Casas of which the diaspora are members. Quantitative research, by way of SurveyMonkey, was conducted (in English, since almost every member of the Macanese community speaks native-level English) via email; thus in this first round an identical set of questions was sent to and received by each informant. It was deemed that engagement was likely to be greater if informants could answer a simple survey, by way of ticking boxes, rather than being required to respond in written sentences. Those who wanted to make further comments or contact me individually were invited to do so. It should be noted that many of the names of respondents have been changed.

This survey was largely disseminated by Casa presidents, with the option to also disseminate a letter from the sponsoring body (IEEM) confirming the credentials of the research and researcher. Some of these presidents are known personally to this author; others were kindly introduced by friends. Unfortunately, there was no success in getting introduced to any Casa in Brazil, and generic emails sent to these Casas did not garner any response. So there were very few responses from Macanese living in Brazil.

It is difficult to know exactly how many people received this survey, as not all presidents offered information on the size of their mailing lists. At least one president privately decided to whom, or otherwise, the survey would be sent. A few of my friends also kindly sent the survey to people who may not be members of a Casa. Further, we know that not all members have email addresses; and we also know that not everyone checks their email inbox regularly. All this said, it is anticipated that the survey reached 1,500–2,000 people. The response rate was anticipated to be around 10 per cent. In fact, 241 responses were received, amounting to a proportion of between 12 per cent and 16 per cent, which is deemed a successful result and a sufficiently robust sampling to produce some reliable data. Further contact via email or in person in Macau should be seen to substantiate or provide development of the survey findings.

One problem with disseminating the survey through the Casas is that it reached Macanese who are already sufficiently engaged with their Macanese-ness to actually join a Macanese association. Further, those who filled out the questionnaire are already those more engaged with their Macanese-ness with particular regard to Macanese cuisine. On the other hand, the author put out a request on LinkedIn, asking for those who identified as Macanese if they would like to take part in a survey to get in contact. One (Chinese) connection sent the message to a Macanese friend (who did not get in contact). Two LinkedIn members—with Chinese family names—came forward, but when asked to supply their email addresses did not respond.

Overall response to the survey was positive, and it met with only one real complaint: one respondent was 'insulted' that s/he could not specify the city of birth (in this case, a city in China); that the question only allowed you to be born in Macau, born overseas, second generation overseas, or with a long family history of living outside Macau. There were quibbles about whether cities in China, or even Hong Kong, counted as 'overseas'. Assuming (knowing) that almost the entirety of respondents were more than twenty years of age, and thus born before the Hong Kong and Macau Handovers in June 1997 and December 1999 respectively, cities in China would count as overseas, with Hong Kong and Macau each deemed to be self-governed until these dates.

Such negative responses, though only one was potentially particularly serious, further serve to raise interesting questions about identity; and thus essentially become part of the research findings. I was alerted to some vague scepticism voiced about the survey, but this allegation was (unfortunately) not substantiated. Let's put that comment down to some kind of gossip, then. But, in the big picture, engagement, lack of engagement, and positions such as scepticism all potentially become part of the 'story' in this kind of research.

Analysis was conducted of subsequent responses. The survey concluded with an invitation to supply this author with a personal email address if respondents wished to continue to take part in the research in a deeper, more detailed manner. The next round of research, then, was personalized emails with further questions targeted around the more striking responses in the survey—for example, if someone strongly agreed that they shared recipes they were asked to expand on this; or if someone strongly disagreed that Macanese cuisine was an important part of their cultural identity they were asked to expand.

Of these 241 respondents, 39 participants not previously known to this author, or about 15 per cent, provided their email addresses. Of these, about half responded to subsequent emails, some in quite some detail, providing valuable and often deeply personal insights.

A parallel survey was conducted among Macanese living in Macau, and informants here included members of the Macanese community actively involved in the catering/hospitality industry. Informants were also of Chinese (or other) ethnicity but limited to those involved in the hospitality industry, thus having a good understanding of how Portuguese and Macanese cuisines are situated within the restaurant industry as part of the dynamic tourism industry. The questionnaire was administered through the Macanese Gastronomy Association in Macau, and also to this author's personal contact list.

Face-to-face interviews were carried out in Macau in the period from 16 to 21 October 2017. These interviews were semi-structured so as to gather both quantitative and qualitative data. In total, there were seven one-on-one interviews with Macanese, one with a Portuguese industry veteran, one with an American industry veteran, and one with a Chinese industry veteran. Other meetings and dinners took place in small groups. Subsequent questionnaires were sent to key industry figures who had not been interviewed in person, in total sixteen of them, of which the response rate was low.

Sample Questions—Quantitative
- Do you identify as Macanese
- How often do you eat Macanese food (once a week, once a month, once a year)
- Do you personally cook Macanese food
- Who is your household cooks Macanese food
- Do you eat Macanese food at home or at gatherings of the Macanese community?
- How often do you visit Macau?

Sample Questions—Qualitative
- How important is Macanese cuisine in terms of your Macanese identity?
- What are your earliest food memories?
- Do you encourage/invite your non-Macanese friends to share Macanese food?
- What is your relationship with Macau? With Portugal?
- Do you consider yourself a global citizen, or as Macanese?
- Do you believe the fact that you are in a Portuguese-speaking country [for informants in Portugal and Brazil] make a difference to your attitude to Macanese food?

Additional research was conducted through recipes (many already in the author's possession) and cookbooks, to see how recipes have been modified across time and space.

Fieldwork in Malaysia

The second tranche of fieldwork was carried out in Malaysia. The decision to broaden the research beyond Macau arose because it emerged that in order to start to understand the nature of Macanese cuisine it has to be seen in a broader Asian context. This applies to Portuguese culinary influence across Asia, but also to observable intra-Asian culinary conversations. Fieldwork was undertaken in Kuala Lumpur and Malacca from 17 to 21 July 2018, and involved meeting and talking with, in mostly informal circumstances, members of the Peranakan (Nyonya-Baba), the Malay, the Chinese, and the Kristang communities. It involved sharing the food of all these communities and, in the case of the latter three, cooking alongside chefs. It involved visits to restaurants, markets, villages and neighbourhoods, and museums.

Appendix 2
Diaspora and the Casa Movement

> Macau has a persona that leaves a picture almost frozen in time that this last generation recaptures when thinking of this charmed reverie they are leaving or have left behind. (Jorge da Silva 2015, 119)

> Diaspora: The dispersion or spread of any people from their original homeland (Oxford English Dictionary)

Introduction: What Is the Macanese Diaspora?

Unlike the majority, the Macanese diaspora is not critically an economic process. Some Macanese may have moved overseas for education or for professional opportunity, but most have left for social and cultural reasons[1] (and even as some have anecdotally regretted that decision). So the volition has not been to send remittances home. In Macau, economic change and development in the home region are almost exclusively brought about as a result of government initiatives to improve the economy. A further contrast to note is that it was from the early 2000s onwards that the economy was such that Macanese (or anyone who had been born in Macau, of course) were now the first generation to have the option to return to Macau to pursue their careers after education or who were not required to leave in the first place. Those involved in the hospitality industry, for example, attests to this.

For a detailed understanding of the Macanese diaspora across time, see such comprehensive texts as João de Pina-Cabral's *Between China and Europe: Person, Culture and Emotion in Macao* (2002), and *Macaenses: The Portuguese in China* by Antonio M. Jorge da Silva (2015); also see the References for further details. But for a deeper understanding of its process in relation to this particular piece of research, a few points should be stressed here. First, it should be noted that the Macanese would have historically inhabited the middle of three tiers as a distinct ethnic group: not quite Portuguese, but certainly not Chinese who had historically (but only historically, and certainly not in the last 100 years) sat on the bottom rung in Macau. Further, there is no single Macanese community. João de Pina-Cabral describes a mode of snobbery that can be encountered in Macanese circles. 'Those persons and families who retain the greater capital of Portuguese-ness—locally known as "traditional" families—as well as those that are richer and/or more educated are prone to discriminate against poorer, less educated families and against people whose family origin is based on a recent intermarriage between a Chinese woman and a Portuguese man' (Pina-Cabral 2002, 145).

Those families who left for the Foreign Concessions in treaty port cities such as Shanghai would have enjoyed something of the privilege of the expatriate—though later they would also become culturally 'more Chinese'. Those in Hong Kong would have also enjoyed a certain status, and were here considered Portuguese, though they would have felt a distinct subordination to the British colonialists. But when Macanese left for Australia, for Canada, for America, they would be abandoning colonial-style lifestyles and a sense of belonging, and becoming just another ethnic group; but one that no one had heard of, and coming from a place which no one had heard of. 'Prior to the diaspora no one then asked where they were from; within their community, they were either Macau-Portuguese, Hong Kong-Portuguese, or Shanghai-Portuguese. Few of the Portuguese community in Hong Kong and Shanghai before the diaspora identified themselves socially as Macaense or Macanese; they were always proud to be identified as Portuguese' (Jorge da Silva 2015, 183).

Unless they were moving to a Portuguese-speaking country, these diasporic Macanese were not able to slip easily into a Portuguese identity. For example, the existing Portuguese community in California was mainly made up of agricultural immigrants from the Azores, with whom the well-educated Macanese on arrival, it has been argued, had little or nothing in common (Jorge da Silva 2015, 181).

The first key wave of diaspora was around 1845, following the cessation of Hong Kong to the British. British companies and merchants had previously been based in Macau, with Macanese in their employ. These Macanese, working in government positions and for institutions such as the Hongkong and Shanghai Banking Corporation (HSBC), moved to Hong Kong, and 'Macau receded into the background of their lives' (Jorge da Silva 2015, 138). There was even a residential area just above Central, in what is now known as Soho, peopled almost entirely by the Portuguese (Macanese), within walking distance of their own space, Club Lusitano. In the 1940s, the dual forces of European wartimes and the emerging of a new China brought much instability, and many decided to leave, seeking a better life. Riots in Hong Kong and Macau in the 1960s caused further instability for non-Chinese. Macanese also started to leave for university beyond the colleges of Portugal, but into English-speaking countries.

The final straw, perhaps, came in the mid-1980s when Margaret Thatcher began negotiations for the return to China of Hong Kong and the New Territories, causing the dramatic so-called Brain Drain in Hong Kong, with families moving overseas (particularly to Canada) to have their children educated elsewhere. Hong Kong's reversion to China took place a dozen or so years later, in 1997. The writing was on the wall for Macau and its own, somewhat perilous, relationship with China. Negotiations began, and the Portuguese administration bade its own farewell in December 1999.

And so to Portugal

Would the Macanese have made the more obvious decision to go to Portugal? Although all residents of Macau were granted Portuguese passports, this did not necessarily equate to the right to citizenship. At this historical juncture, it should be noted that the Macanese were descendants of the Portuguese: it was not as if they had a country to 'return to'. In any event, the relationship with Portugal was somewhat complicated. Alexander Mamak discussed how 'race' as such had not been deemed important, as compared with the broader culture, including cuisine, which had been handed down over generations; and notions of Portuguese-ness were highly nuanced. 'The glue that holds the original Macanese together is a common religious and a deep affinity with Portugal, *a country which many have never seen*. Their *symbolic* world with respect to food and other aspects of culture is Portuguese' (Mamak 2007, 162) (my italics).

Additionally, many Macanese in the diaspora left because they already felt that they had 'lost' Macau; that how it exists in memory is markedly different to its contemporary incarnation(s).

> 'I was there on a short business trip and so much has changed that I don't feel it's the Macau I used to enjoy visiting anymore.' —Vitor Souza (personal correspondence, November 2017)

Once seeing themselves as sons of the land, the indigenous people, they feel that the place has been stolen from them; that they are a displaced people; that they can never return to their Macau. Yet it must be questioned as to whether Macau ever did 'belong' to the Macanese in more than an imagined way. Today, familiar, evocative Macau architectural landmarks, such as São Domingo's Church, the Leal and Largo Senado, and the Guia Lighthouse, are all under the banner of UNESCO heritage status, transforming them from being part of the local landscape to being part of a global movement. They're now part of a tourism package, too, which changes their meaning still further. We are reminded of the idea, or the sense, 'that in preserving you are freezing, or even killing' (Sutton 2001, 171).

My own research has further suggested that there is no single, contemporary sense of Macanese-ness. I received comments such as: 'I guess I am a misfit. My parents had bad experiences with nuns and priests . . . so I got sent to a non-religious school in Shanghai . . . [my mother] wasn't comfortable at the Club Lusitano [in Hong Kong], so my father attended functions alone' (personal correspondence, November 2017). James Nobre shared that: 'it's likely the early uprooting of both myself and a lot of the Macanese that I never had a very close connection with the Macanese community' (personal correspondence, November 2017). And this comment from someone living in Macau: 'Perhaps the definition of a Macanese identity is very plural and diversified' (personal correspondence, November 2017).

Macanese in the diaspora

One of the key intentions of this research was to explore if, or to what extent, the Macanese in the diaspora exhibit a different relationship to Macanese cuisine as compared to those who live in Macau. As has been noted above, however, there is no such thing as a single diaspora. The idea for the research was the fact that there are now more Macanese living outside Macau than within. Without a critical mass of Macanese in Macau, could a cuisine potentially become a museum piece in the place wherein it was born? Does it, or could it, engage in transformative processes in its new geographical context(s) so as to have little culturally in common with its motherland?

According to the findings of a survey carried out during 2013, the estimation was made that there was a global total of 198,105 people who identified as Macanese, dispersed among thirty-five regions and countries.[2] This figure was immediately contested on the same website by Macanese writer Jim Silva who, in addition to writing that 'the definition of who is "Macanese" is still being debated', posited that the actual figure would probably be 10 per cent of this, and that 80 per cent of those were living beyond Macau, Hong Kong, and Shanghai.

'Based on new research and an extrapolation of data from recent surveys, the current population of Macanese around the world is estimated at more than 1.5 million.'[3] A definition of what constitutes Macanese is offered: 'We define "Macanese" broadly as either: 1) Portuguese Eurasians born in Macau; or 2) the descendants of Portuguese Eurasians (Luso-Asians) with cultural roots in Portugal, Goa, and western India, Macau, Hong Kong, Canton, Shanghai, Japan, Malaysia, Indonesia, or Timor.'[4]

'Portuguese genealogist Dr. Jorge Forjaz has identified over 50,000 Macanese family names. Several thousand more names will be added to a revised edition to Forjaz's 1996 publication, due out in 2017. Other researchers in Europe and Southeast Asia, citing archival data from Goa, Malaysia, Thailand, Timor, and the Philippines, suggest that number may include at least 10,000 more family names, given the historical prevalence of inter-marriage and adoption by other ethnic groups.'[5]

In Macau itself, estimates of how many Macanese live there are no more than estimates—with figures varying from 3,500 and between 10,000 and 20,000 mooted. It is suggested that this figure fell as low as 7,000 in 2001 (Eusebio 2013). The Macau population is 615,000, with women outnumbering men, but there are no official census figures dividing the population by ethnicity/nationality. What is certain is that there are more Macanese living outside Macau than within.

Macau's Changing Fortunes and Identities

'Unfortunately, Macau has an identity problem.' —Ivo Guterres (personal correspondence, November 2017)

Migration of Macanese has consisted of a number of significant waves, all set against the backdrop of a city with constantly changing identities. Following the first

Portuguese arrivals in 1511, Macau grew so significantly in wealth that it become known as the so-called Venice of the East—and is again hugely wealthy today, though now, of course, compared to Vegas rather than Venice.[6] 'Until the nineteenth century Macao was just a transit city for foreigners and Portuguese from the mainland, and although the Chinese afforded the city its character, its soul lay with the Macaenses (Macanese) or "sons of the land"' (Pons 1999, 100).

Things would change after the cessation of nearby Hong Kong to the British in 1841 and this process, coupled by the rapid development of Shanghai, preceded a wave of Macanese migration. As David Brookshaw wrote in his introduction to the novel *The Bewitching Braid* by Henrique de Senna Fernandes: 'They took with them their language and cultural traditions, establishing "Oriental Portuguese" diasporas in Hong Kong, Shanghai, Guangzhou and the other port cities of China' (De Senna Fernandes 2004). But the 1920s and 1930s, Brookshaw further notes, 'were decades when the Macanese felt secure, unaware of the great upheavals that were to come, when their culinary arts were practised by the old families and patuá was still spoken among an older generation' (Brookshaw 2004, ix).

In a reaction to the disruptions of the Second World War, some Macanese emigrated to Hong Kong where there were jobs; and to countries in the West, in particular to Portugal; and to other Portuguese-speaking countries including Mozambique, Angola, and Brazil. They went for education, for employment, or a fresh start. According to Antonia Jorge da Silva, 'This was the turning point in the lives of many Macaense families' (Jackson 2003, xi) with the swell of migration. As Brookshaw explained it, 'The older Macanese families . . . [were] convinced that the city's days of Portuguese rule over their tiny homeland were numbered, and that Macao was destined to be surrendered to China at some point in the near future' (de Senna Fernandes 2004, viii).

This 'surrender' was of course not to occur until 1999, and it was during the run up to this event that many more Macanese families felt abandoned by the Macau government, some fearfully convinced that they were becoming stateless. By now, the Macanese community was beginning to move all over the world, to English-speaking countries such as Canada, the USA, and Australia.

What we begin to see is the emergence of a community—the Macanese—now beginning to define themselves as an ethnically (and possibly culturally) distinct group. The consequential waves of movement show 'the ways that globalisation and local identity are closely related processes' (Wilk 2002, 68) and, he begins to argue, they are not necessarily in opposition. One fights for distinction, perhaps, in the face of a wave of homogeneity.

It would appear that the first widely circulated canon of Macanese recipes beyond intimate family circles was created because of diaspora, critically among the community who left for Shanghai who were fighting for identity and social position. Suddenly, Macanese 'cuisine' became a critical identifier of difference and cohesion. This idea that Macanese cooking became a foodway, a culinary entity, only in the diaspora mirrors the observations of Claudia Roden, writing about the Jews of Italy, regarding what might be understood as 'Jewish cuisine'. 'Most importantly it was their mobility and the impact of Jewish immigrants from abroad that made Jewish food distinctive.'[7]

The Casa Movement

'If I had stayed in Macau, I am not sure if I would have realised how important it is to keep my own Macanese-ness alive, nor recognised how fragile is the Macanese identity. In Macau, it is much easier to take Macanese-ness for granted ... I would say that the Macanese who have lived overseas might feel stronger about maintaining their Macanese identity compared to those in Macau. However, I also know that after the Handover in 1999, there were many Macanese who went through the experience of feeling displaced—and perhaps still do.'—Isabel da Silva (Jackson 2003, 26)

This research began with the question of whether attitudes to cultural identity through food, in particular, significantly vary between the diaspora, as compared with Macanese who are resident in Macau. Isabel's statement, above, may nuance this binary separation. Isabel left Macau as a teenager for her education. She felt very much the 'other' at boarding school in the UK; then moved to Australia where she lived with members of her extended Macanese family, and consolidated her sense of Macanese-ness. She returned to Macau as a young adult in the 1990s, fortunate enough to find good employment. Thus she had lived in a country where there was no Macanese community, and then in a country with a burgeoning sense of community, and finally back to Macau where Macanese-ness might be seen to be 'taken for granted'.

The diaspora visits Macau: The Encontro

The main events held in Macau in December 2016 at the most recent 'Encontro das Comunidades Macaenses' (the Macanese Community Meeting held every three years for the Macanese diaspora) included a conference featuring a number of speakers, a visit to the UNESCO World Heritage Historic Centre, including the St. Joseph Seminary, a trip to neighbouring Guangzhou, a mass at the cathedral and, of course food events. For example, the Macanese Cha Gordo feast was organised by the Brotherhood of Macanese Gastronomy, with the assistance of a number of Macanese cooks/chefs.

These meetings, which began in 1993, are semi-government subsidised, and the Macau Chief Executive (at this event Chief Executive Chui Sai On) gives an address. 'These Encontros (meetings), which could be seen as "gathering of the clans" or "homecoming", brought both cheers and tears to the ageing members of the worldwide community' (Jorge da Silva 2015, 202).

Meetings are also held for the 'Youth Encontro', the majority of whom would have been born outside Macau, in order to enhance—or ignite—their sense of Macanese identity; or simply to have the chance to visit the land of their ancestors. Several comments have been about the lack of interest among the younger Macanese in exploring their Macanese culture, owing to a process of acculturation, such as this one:

> 'From my experience, many 2nd generation Macanese overseas are largely disconnected from their cultural identity and tend to see themselves as part of the new country/culture they are settled in with very little connection to the physical place of Macau. —Johann Almeida (personal correspondence, November 2017)

In past years (2004 and 2007), when there was 'more money sloshing around' (to quote one respondent), cooking competitions have also been a focus. They started as cooking competitions within each Casa, with the subsequent winners competing against each other in Macau, where they were judged by a panel of prominent local Macanese. In 2007, Martin Yan was invited by the Casa of San Francisco to attend. Apparently, he went on to cook a Macanese dish on mainstream US TV cooking show *Yan Can Cook*.

The highly competitive nature of these competitions is also indicative of the strong relationship between a family and the family's recipes. Competitiveness is 'in their blood' said one respondent.

> 'In the Macanese cuisine heritage there was always this "thing" of "my family recipe is better than yours", so when you have a competition going on it is always about families in a way. Of course there is also a strong and fierce conviction that each competitor is the best cook: they are very proud of their cooking skills.' —Hugo Bandeira, lecturer and F&B Manager, IFT (personal correspondence, December 2017)

Such statements about competition among families do not seem to suggest any unpleasantness within that sense of competitiveness. Rather, there is the suggestion of friendly rivalry; and indeed the Macanese tend to joke about and tease each other (personal observation) but only gently. Interestingly, the atmosphere in the kitchen at the Finals—in this case the teaching kitchens of the Institute of Tourism Studies (IFT)—are noted as reminiscent of the home kitchen, with intergenerational transmission of knowledge.

> 'It was a lot of fun and no one was fighting each other, very cordial gathering in the kitchen, like the old days the old ladies teach the younger generation.' —Luis Machado, Head of the Macanese Gastronomy Association (personal correspondence, December 2017)

However, it is noted that the atmosphere within each Casa may have been 'aggressive', notes one informant, since the prize for the winner was a pair of return air tickets. Antonia Tsai, who represented the Casa de Macau no Toronto in 2004, says that contestants took the competition very seriously and that some tension did exist, but it was more of a 'friendly competitiveness' (personal correspondence, 2017).

There is little question of how important these meetings are for the preservation and celebration of Macanese culture in the community, and the significant role that the Casa movement, and various overseas Macanese organisations, have similarly played.

'I think that besides food, a sense of attachment to Macau as a physical place of origin; regular Encontro trips to Macau; overseas Macanese cultural associations and clubs actively holding cultural events, and Macanese patua language are also very important to my Macanese identity—in that order of importance.' —Johann Almeida (personal correspondence, November 2017)

In 2004, the Council of Macanese Communities (Conselho das Comunidades Macaenses, or CCM) was founded with a remit to manage all the Macanese associations, which now number nineteen. Of these, thirteen are for Macanese in the diaspora, while there are six in Macau (Sales Marques 2017). The first to be opened was 150 years ago, in Central, in downtown Hong Kong: Club Lusitano continues to be successful, though membership criteria regarding Portuguese identity/nationality have relaxed slightly. The restaurant opens daily (Portuguese and Macanese dishes feature on the menu), there's a bar and a library area, several function rooms for outside hire including a ballroom, and there are rooms set aside for leisure activities such as mah-jong. Its importance is illustrated here:

'In Hong Kong our "identity" was much preserved because the Portuguese/Macanese largely married within the community, and everything got anchored by our two clubs, Lusitano and Recreio; and to a lesser extent by employment. I think this became more difficult to maintain as many joined the diaspora and inevitably married outside the community.' —Anthony Cabral (personal correspondence, October 2017)

Its position in the community is rather different to that of other Casas, in that although it is a social club—and indeed was originally established as a 'Gentlemen's Club' (as explained by Club president, Patrick Ozario during a telephone conversation in January 2018). Its geographically central location—in Central—also means that it serves as a venue for business meetings.

Casa de Macau in Portugal was established in 1967, followed by the co-opting of various Casas and clubs in the USA, Canada, Australia, and Brazil. The most recent to be co-opted is the UK's Macau Home, in 2016. The expansion of this movement, as is explored in a discourse on the notion of identity after diaspora, has been because the Macanese were no longer a walk or a bus ride away from friends and family. Because they were 'living away from their familiar community clusters, an initial sense of insecurity and need for cultural consocation came about for some' (Jorge da Silva: 2015, 183).

'Being a member of and participating in activities at Casa de Macau reinforces my sense of belonging to the Macanese community and my cultural heritage.' —Antonia Lai (personal correspondence, November 2017)

For some, the reasons go deeper still, and they stress the importance of family for continuity of identity, in the same way that cooking the recipes of one's mother, of grandmother, are deemed to be so important. Simon Ramos wrote to me to say that he had lost both his parents, as well as his two brothers, and that being sent to boarding school when he was seven years old had already created a sense of disconnect with his family.

> 'The reason I got involved with the Casa was to pay tribute to my family so I can be closer to them.' —Simon Ramos (personal correspondence, November 2017)

Council of Macanese Communities

The CCM sees for itself a role in, for example, helping to promote Macau overseas as a world-class tourist destination, but critically it wants to enhance communication among the Casas, and between the Casas and government or quasi-government bodies in Macau. It wants to help to attract younger members of the Macanese community, and to promote the learning of Portuguese and Chinese. The ability to speak the three languages most commonly used by Macanese—Portuguese, Chinese and English—has been cited as a signifier of cultural identity by some informants. Such factors are clearly important for the continuation and strengthening of Macanese identity, but food (and traditions, which may be around food) remains central. In the course of diaspora, the patuá was lost. The traditional ability to move easily between English, Portuguese, and Cantonese was lost (indeed only a handful of informants said their key language of communication at home was Cantonese), and a unity through the traditions of Catholicism was lost. The cooking remains.

In a personal conversation in Macau in October 2017 with Isabela Costa, she commented that she only knew a single word of patuá. 'Macanese food keeps us proud of our heritage. The Chinese have their version, but that doesn't make the Chinese experts in Macanese cuisine. Without Macanese food, what? Patuá?'

Notes

Introduction
1. The Macau population census of 2011 showed that out of a population of 552,503, 92.3 per cent were Chinese and 6.8 per cent 'Other'. Only 0.9 per cent of respondents identified as Portuguese. It is notable that a significant proportion—2.7 per cent—of this group were Filipino, who are principally employed in hospitality and catering, or work as domestic helpers.
2. International Conference on Foodways and Heritage: A Perspective of Safeguarding Intangible Cultural Heritage, jointly organized by the Hong Kong Heritage Museum, Leisure and Cultural Services Department, Department of Anthropology, The Chinese University of Hong Kong and the UNESCO Chair project on Safeguarding and Promoting Cultural Food Heritage of Tours University, France.
3. See, for example, Kershen 2002.
4. After French sociologist Pierre Bourdieu's notion of *habitus*.
5. Peter Gordon enacted fusion brilliantly in The Sugar Club in London in the 1990s—carpaccio of kangaroo with Thai fish sauce and torn coriander leaves is one strong memory. But a lemon grass-flavoured risotto in a one-star Michelin restaurant in Turin in 2012 was just irritating.
6. This book will question whether Macanese cooking was indeed something unique, something entirely new, or something more hybrid or fused.

Chapter 1
1. Torrada de Queizo is a Portuguese translation. In Macau they sometimes appear as Tostas de Queijo. Shrimp Toasts are sometimes called Tostas de Camarão and also as Vivienne's Har Toasy (see, for example, Jackson 2003, 50). Har is the Cantonese word for shrimp; and toasy sounds very much like a Cantonese pronunciation of toast, in the manner of Minchi (based on the English words mince or minced). So these shrimps toasts may well have been created in the kitchens of Club de Recreio by a Cantonese cook—quite possibly with the given or assumed name of Vivienne.
2. See Appendix 2 for a description of the Casa movement.

Chapter 2
1. For information about the Encontro, see Appendix 2.
2. I carried out a very informal research in August 2018 into what might be the 'national' dish of Macau. I started with a question about Hong Kong, to which almost all respondents

mentioned the intrinsically Cantonese dim sum or char sui. For Macau, the first response was egg tarts (pastéis de nata). However, as academic Manual Noronha confirmed, it really depends who you are as to how you might respond. 'From the local Chinese perspective, it will have to be "Portuguese" Chicken. From the Macanese perspective, it will definitely by Tacho, and from the tourists: egg tarts or the Macau "Prego" Pork-chop Buns".' In the past, Hong Kong Cantonese might have gone to Macau for Cantonese dishes that were no longer available in Hong Kong. Such dishes are probably not available in Macau either these days.

3. Source: Macau Government Tourism Office (personal communication, August 2018).
4. An excerpt from a poem written by Jose dos Santos Ferreira, originated in the Macau patuá and is here translated into English. It was written ten years before Handover, in anticipation of those who identified as Macanese having to/choosing to leave Macau (Jorge da Silva 2015, 201).
5. Hutton 2007.
6. Apparently Flamingo has now been reopened on its original spot, in the hotel that is now known as The Regency, though as at June 2019 this has yet to be verified.

Chapter 3

1. Thomas Keller is a prominent starred and award-winning American chef, the proprietor of The French Laundry in Napa Valley and Per Se in Manhattan.
2. Antonia Lai, who lives in Toronto, has taken the dish yet further. She shared with me that she combines ground veal with the pork; and has further modified her recipe in order to enrich flavours and textures; she even adds oatmeal to increase the fibre content.
3. Tik yau is the first extraction of fermented soybeans, which is generally regarded as a superior kind of sutate (soy sauce).
4. Graça Pacheco Jorge is the author of Macanese cookbook *A Cozinha de Macau de Casa do Meu Avô*.
5. Antonio Jorge da Silva has touched on the subject of rivalry in *Macaenses: The Portuguese in China* (2015), and how friendly rivalry can have its darker side. He has said that he was criticised for writing about this (personal correspondence, January 2018).
6. From *Accounting for Taste: The Triumph of French Cuisine* (2004), as cited in Buccafusco 2007.
7. http://en.macaotourism.gov.mo/dining/recipes.php.
8. http://www.macaneselibrary.org/PublicE-o/uicuisineenglish.htm.
9. It should be noted that 'niche' cookbooks get a limited print-run and recipe books with colour photography are expensive to produce, without enjoying any economies of scale. It should also be noted that there are some excellent Macanese cookbooks in existence, and I would particularly single out two (note that I can only refer to the English-language cookbooks that I have seen, as I don't read Portuguese or Chinese). First, *Macanese Cooking: A Journey Across Generations* by Cecilia Jorge, which has been published (in Macau by APIM, 2004) in three languages: English, Portuguese, and Chinese. She has done tremendous work on researching the derivation of dishes through, for example, examining the names of dishes. Secondly, *Macaense Cuisine: Origins and Evolution* by Antonio M. Jorge da Silva (published in Macau by IIM, 2016) in which he has attempted to place particular recipes within the decades, thus illustrating how recipes might have been adapted over time.

Chapter 4

1. I am grateful to London-based restaurateur and chef Vivek Singh (The Cinnamon Club in Westminster, among others) for introducing me to this cow's milk cheese, as well as to a curd known in India as Chhena, which would have been utilised by the Portuguese and Portuguese-descendants in the making of desserts.
2. Dodol is also a sweetmeat in Malaysia and Sri Lanka—sometimes said to have been brought to Sri Lanka by Malaysian immigrants.
3. http://www.damanonline.in/city-guide/food-in-daman (accessed 13 January 2018).
4. Her subsequent analysis of why it was France that developed gastronomically and not Italy centres on the importance of having a centrally recognised institution; in this case the French court.
5. Many thanks to UK-based chef Norman Musa, who comes from Penang, for first introducing me to this sauce, which I went on to experience at lunchtime in Malacca.
6. Infamous in the United Kingdom, Vindaloo was for decades seen as the most spicy curry on Indian restaurant menus, and became associated with heavy drinking sessions and 'dares'.

Chapter 5

1. There is a renowned Portuguese-Macanese restaurant named A Lorcha close to A-Ma Temple in Macau, serving as a fitting monument to the unique style of boat; and examples of it can also be seen in the ethnographical Museum of Macau and in the Maritime Museum.
2. As included in Jorge da Silva (2015, 48), citing Almerindo Lessa in *A Historia e os Homens da Primeira Republica Deomocrata do Oriente*.
3. The term 'Eurasian' may be problematic. It is often taken to refer to someone who has one Asian parent and one European parent when the reality may be more 'mixed' than that, with the Macanese being a good example. The Macanese may represent a 'coherent' community in ethnic terms, but other communities may not be thus. So to make a distinction between, for example, the Dutch burghers of Sri Lanka and the Portuguese burghers of Sri Lanka is seen as important. Further, Malaysian 'Eurasians', for example, distinguish themselves geographically (ergo culturally) from Singaporean 'Eurasians'. See Duruz (2016) for further discussion on such terminology.
4. 20 piculs is equivalent to about 1,200 kg.
5. Tan Chee-Beng, who conducted long-term research among the Baba, says it may be convenient to use the concept of hybridisation relating to Baba culture, but that it generates sweeping assumptions that may not stand up. 'In the case of Nyonya cuisine, it is more helpful to study it as a product of cultural localization, arising from Chinese and non-Chinese cultural interaction in the context of the Malayan environment' (Tan 2007, 171–72).
6. Keluak is a large tree nut, somewhat resembling a black walnut, which is native to the mangrove swamps of South East Asia. It is a distinctive ingredient in the cooking of Malacca and best-known in Nyonya-Baba cooking. It is quite complicated and time-consuming to prepare.
7. It is pointed out that the term 'Macanese', the English rendering of the Portuguese 'Macaense', has been a relatively recent linguistic development, relating specifically to the diaspora. 'Few of the Portuguese community in Hong Kong and Shanghai before the diaspora identified themselves socially as Macaense or Macanese; they were always proud to be identified as Portuguese' (Jorge da Silva 2015, 183).

8. A large majority of Chinese in Macau and Hong Kong identify as 'Macau-Chinese' or 'Hong Kong-ese'; and the relationship between them and mainland Chinese has become (mutually) strained in the last two decades or so, particularly since mainland Chinese began to travel in volume to Hong Kong and Macau.
9. *Lights and Shadows of a Macao Life 1829–34*.
10. The term amah is today generalised to refer to a female domestic helper. Its origins are contested, though widely believed to have come either from the Portuguese *ama* (nurse) or from the Chinese ah ma (little mother, or grandmother). For a more detailed explanation, see Constable (2007).
11. An American cultural anthropologist (1926–2006), Geertz argued that the practice of thick description could provide sufficient cultural context for a person beyond that culture to derive meaning from, and understand, actions, or words, and so on.
12. This patuá has all but died out now, though is seeing something of a revival through the performances of the Doci Papiacam di Macau, the only theatre group performing in this endangered creole (Eusebio 2013).
13. http://kravingsfoodadventures.com/goan-masala-kheema.

Conclusion

1. This has been named as the most reviewed bakery in the world: https://www.businessinsider.com/pasteis-de-belem-bakery-in-lisbon-is-the-most-reviewed-eatery-in-the-world-2018-1?r=US&IR=T (accessed 26 January 2019).
2. Pastéis de nata was introduced to Macau in 1986, at the former Hyatt Regency hotel on Taipa, by pastry chef Elias da Silva. It has since become an iconic food item across Macau.
3. French sociologist Pierre Bourdieu's theory of *habitus* refers to his idea that deeply engrained (daily) habits represent a physical embodiment of culture.
4. Imagine, as an extreme example, a Minchi station in the 'coffee shop' of a five-star hotel in Macau, where you can choose your own ratio of ground beef to pork; of dark soy to light soy; and possibly even omit Lea & Perrins altogether and choose kecap manis instead.

Appendix 2

1. Anabel de Souza, a Macanese woman whom I interviewed in Macau in October 2017, further nuanced the nature of the diaspora, and I believe her comments may shed some light on some aspects of the disposition of the Macanese people. She said: 'We are not a united people, we love to fight with each other. If we were united, we would have more people in our own town.' She added that there were more Filipinos living and working in Macau than Macanese (she put the number at 6,000 Filipinos versus 3,500 Macanese). Her suggestion is perhaps echoed by Tony da Silva: 'We are a very complex group of people' (personal correspondence, November 2017).
2. Source: www.macstudies.net (accessed 2014).
3. Source: www.macstudies.net (accessed December 2017).
4. Source: www.macstudies.net (accessed December 2017).
5. Source: www.macstudies.net (accessed December 2017).
6. One can wryly note that the memory of Venice is unwittingly preserved with the gondolas at The Venetian hotel and casino on Cotai strip.
7. See http://www.zamir.org/Features/Italy/RodenFood.shtml (accessed 24 March 2019)

References

Appadurai, Arjun. 1988. 'How to Make a National Cuisine: Cookbooks in Contemporary India'. *Comparative Studies in Society and History* 30, no. 1 (1988): 3–24.

Augustin-Jean, Louis. 2002. 'Food Consumption, Food Perception and the Search for a Macanese Identity'. In *The Globalisation of Chinese Food*, edited by David Wu and Sidney Cheung, 113–27. London: RoutledgeCurzon.

Avieli, Nir. 2012. *Rice Talks: Food and Community in a Vietnamese Town*. Bloomington: Indiana University Press.

Beattie, Sarah. 2014. *Meat-Free Any Day: Food for All Reasons*. Bournemouth, England: Select Publisher Services.

Belasco, Warren. 2005. 'Food and the Counterculture'. In *The Cultural Politics of Food and Eating*, edited by James Watson and Melissa Caldwell, 217–34. Oxford: Wiley-Blackwell.

Black, Maggie. 1992. *The Medieval Cookbook*. New York: Thames and Hudson.

Borges, Charles, and Helmut Feldmann. 1997. *Goa and Portugal: Their Cultural Links*. New Delhi: Concept Publishing.

Boxer, Charles Ralph. 1968. *Fidalgos in the Far East 1550–1770*. Oxford: Oxford University Press.

Braga, Stuart. 2012. 'Making Impressions: The Adaptation of a Portuguese Family to Hong Kong, 1700–1950'. PhD diss., The Australian National University.

Brookshaw, David. 2002. *Visions of China: Stories from Macau*. Hong Kong: Hong Kong University Press.

Buccafusco, Christopher. 2007. 'On the Legal Consequences of Sauces: Should Thomas Keller's Recipe Be Per Se Copyrightable'. 24 *Cardozo Arts & Entertainment Law Journal* 1121: 1122–55.

Byrne, John. 2012. 'The Luso-Asians and Other Eurasians: Their Domestic and Diasporic Identities'. In *Culture and Identity in the Luso-Asian World: Tenacities and Plasticities*, edited by Laura Jarnagin, 131–54. Singapore: Institute of Southeast Asian Studies.

Caldicott, Chris, and Carolyn Caldicott. 2001. *The Spice Routes: Chronicles and Recipes from around the World*. London: Frances Lincoln.

Chua, Bee Lia, Razif Aman, Mohiddin Othman, and Hamdin Salleh. 2011. 'Food Image, Satisfaction and Behavioral Intentions: The Case of Malaysia's Portuguese Cuisine'. International CHRIE Conference-Refereed Track.

Chua, Beng Huat, and Ananda Rajah. 2001. 'Hybridity, Ethnicity and Food in Singapore'. In *Changing Chinese Foodways in Asia*, edited by David Y. H. Wu and Chee-Beng Tan, 161–97. Hong Kong: Chinese University Press.

Clammer, John. 1980. *Straits Chinese Society: Studies in the Sociology of the Baba Communities of Malaysia and Singapore*. Singapore: Singapore University Press.
Clark, Priscilla. 1975. 'Thought for Food, I: French Cuisine and French Culture'. *The French Review* XLIX, no. 1: 32–41.
Collingham, Lizzie. 2006. *Curry: A Tale of Cooks and Conquerors*. London: Vintage Books.
Conlon, Abe, and Adrienne Lo. 2016. *The Adventures of Fat Rice: Recipes from the Chicago Restaurant Inspired by Macau*. New York: Ten Speed Press.
Constable, Nicole. 2007. *Maid to Order in Hong Kong: Stories of Migrant Workers*. New York: Cornell University Press.
da Silva Gracias, Fátima. 1997. 'The Impact of Portuguese Culture on Goa: A Myth or a Reality?' In *Goa and Portugal: Their Cultural Links*, edited by Charles Borges and Helmut Feldmann, 39–51. New Delhi: Concept Publishing.
Davidson, Alan. 1999. *The Oxford Companion to Food*. Oxford and New York: Oxford University Press.
Davis, Hilary, Bjorn Nansen, Frank Vetere, Toni Robertson, Margot Brereton, Jeanette Durick, and Kate Vaisutis. 2014. *Homemade Cookbooks: A Recipe for Sharing*. ACM: New York.
de Pina-Cabral, João. 2002. *Between China and Europe: Person, Culture and Emotion in Macao*. London: Continuum.
de Senna Fernandes, Henrique. 2002. 'Candy'. In *Visions of China: Stories from Macau*, edited by David Brookshaw, 97–152. Hong Kong: Hong Kong University Press.
de Senna Fernandes, Henrique. 2004. *The Bewitching Braid*. Hong Kong: Hong Kong University Press.
de Silva Jayasuriya, Shihan. 2008. *The Portuguese in the East: A Cultural History of a Maritime Trading Empire*. London: I. B. Tauris.
Doling, Annabel. 1994. *Macau on a Plate: A Culinary Journey*. Hong Kong: Roundhouse.
D'Souza, Zubin. 2010. *All India Vegetarian Cookbook: A Subzi-Sutra Containing the Secrets of India's Multi-Regional Vegetarian Cuisine*. New York: YBK Publishers.
Duruz, Jean. 2007. 'From Malacca to Adelaide... Fragments towards a Biography of Cooking, Yearning and Laksa'. In *Food and Foodways in Asia: Resource, Tradition and Cooking*, edited by Sidney Cheung and Chee-Beng Tan, 183–200. Abingdon: Routledge.
Duruz, Jean. 2016. 'Love in a Hot Climate: Foodscapes of Trade, Travel, War and Intimacy'. *Gastronomica: The Journal of Critical Food Studies* 16 (1): 16–27.
Eusebio, Maria. 2013. 'The Voice on the Postcolonial Stage'. *The Newsletter* 64 (Summer): 32–33.
Fernandes, Athos. 1997. 'Influence of Portuguese Language and Culture of Daman'. In *Goa and Portugal: Their Cultural Links*, edited by Charles Borges and Helmut Feldmann, 220–33. New Delhi: Concept Publishing.
Fernandes, Joyce. 1990 *Goan Cookbook*. Goa: Self-published.
Fernandis, Gerard. 2003. 'The Portuguese Community at the Periphery: A Minority Report on the Portuguese Quest for *Bumiputera* Status'. *Kajian Malaysia* 1 & 2: 285–301.
Freedman, P. 2008. *Out of the East: Spices and Medieval Cuisine*. New Haven: Yale University Press.
Gonoi, Takashi. 1997. 'Relations between Japan and Goa in the 16th and 17th Centuries'. In *Goa and Portugal: Their Cultural Links*, edited by Charles Borges and Helmut Feldmann, 101–10. New Delhi: Concept Publishing.

Halikowski Smith, Stefan. 2012. 'Eighteenth-Century Diplomatic Relations between Portuguese Macao and Ayutthaya: The 1721 Debt Repayment Embassy from Macao'. In *Culture and Identity in the Luso-Asian World: Tenacities and Plasticities*, edited by Laura Jarnagin, 83–105. Singapore: Institute of Southeast Asian Studies.
Hall, Stuart. 1992. *Modernity and Its Futures*. Cambridge: Polity Press.
Hamilton, Cherie. 2008. *Cuisines of Portuguese Encounters*. New York: Hippocrene Books Inc.
Holtzman, Jon. 2006. 'Food and Memory'. *The Annual Review of Anthropology* 35: 361–78.
Hutton, Wendy. 2007. *The Food of Love: Four Centuries of East-West Cuisine*. Singapore: Marshall Cavendish.
Jackson, Annabel. 2003. *Taste of Macau: Portuguese Cuisine on the China Coast*. Hong Kong: Hong Kong University Press.
James, Allison. 1997. 'How British Is British Food?' In *Food, Health and Identity*, edited by Pat Caplan, 71–86. London: Routledge.
Jorge, Cecilia. 2004. *Macanese Cooking: A Journey across Generations*. Macau: APIM.
Jorge da Silva, Antonio. 2015. *Macaenses: The Portuguese in China*. Macau: Instituto Internacional Macau.
Jorge da Silva, Antonio. 2016. *Macaense Cuisine: Origins and Evolution*. Macau: Instituto Internacional Macau.
Kershen, Anne. 2002. *Food in the Migrant Experience*. London: Routledge.
Kong Weng Hang, Hilary du Cros, and Chin-Ee Ong. 2015. 'Tourism Destination Image Development: A Lesson from Macau'. *International Journal of Tourism Cities* 1 (4): 1–17. http://kravingsfoodadventures.com/goan-masala-kheema/ (accessed August 2017).
Levi, Joseph. 2014. *Macau's Foodscape: Identity within Two Worlds*. The George Washington University.
Low, Harriett. 2002. *Lights and Shadows of a Macao Life: The Journal of Harriett Low, Travelling Spinster*. Washington, WA: The History Bank.
Mamak, Alexander. 2007. 'In Search of a Macanese Cookbook'. In *Food and Foodways in Asia: Resource, Tradition and Cooking*, edited by Sidney Cheung and Chee-Beng Tan, 159–70. Abingdon: Routledge.
Mintz, Sidney. 1996. *Tasting Food, Tasting Freedom: Excursions into Eating, Culture and the Past*. Boston: Beacon.
Mintz, Sidney. 2007. 'Asia's Contributions to World Cuisine'. In *Food and Foodways in Asia: Resource, Tradition and Cooking*, edited by Sidney Cheung and C. B. Tan, 201–10. Abingdon: Routledge.
Mintz, Sidney. 2008. 'Food & Diaspora'. *Food, Culture & Society* 11 (4): 509–23.
Mohd Zulhilmi Suhaimi, and Mohd Salehuddin Mohd Zahari. 2014. 'Common Acceptable Cuisine in Multicultural Countries: Towards Building the National Food Identity'. *International and Scientific Research & Innovation* 8 (3): 855–61.
Musa, Norman. 2016. *Amazing Malaysian: Recipes for Vibrant Malaysian Home Cooking*. London: Square Peg.
Nadkarni, Esha. 2017. 'An Analysis of Portuguese Influence on Goan Cuisine'. *The Expression* 3, no. 4 (August): 319–22.
Ng, Chien Yang, and Shahrim Ab Karim. 2016. 'Historical and Contemporary Perspectives of the Nyonya Food Culture in Malaysia'. *Journal of Ethnic Foods* 3: 93–106.
Nunis, Melba. 2014. *A Kristang Family Cookbook*. Singapore: Marshall Cavendish.

Nurmufida, Muthia, Gervasius Wangrimen, Risty Reinalta, and Leonardi, Kevin. 2017. 'Rendang: The Treasure of Minangkabau'. *Journal of Ethnic Foods* 4, no. 4 (December): 232–35.

Palmer, Robin. 1977. 'The Italians: Patterns of Migration to London'. In *Between Two Cultures: Migrants and Minorities in Britain*, edited by James Watson, 242–68. Oxford: Basil Blackwell.

Parkhurst Ferguson, Patricia. 2004. *Accounting for Taste: The Triumph of French Cuisine*. Chicago: The University of Chicago Press.

Pons, Phillipe. 1999. *Macao*. Hong Kong: Hong Kong University Press.

Prichep, D. 2013. 'Fish Sauce: An Ancient Roman Condiment Rises Again'. NPR: *The Salt*, 26 October 2013.

Reejhsinghani, Aroona. 2000. *Delights from Goa*. Mumbai: Jaico Publishing House.

Saifullah Khan, Verity. 1977. 'The Pakistanis: Mirpuri Villagers at Home and in Bradford'. In *Between Two Cultures: Migrants and Minorities in Britain*, edited by James Watson, 37–89. Oxford: Basil Blackwell.

Sales Marques, José. 2017. 'Homecoming'. *Macau News*, 26 January 2017 (accessed online November 2017).

Singh, Vivek. 2014. *Spice at Home*. Bath, UK: Absolute Press.

Sobral, José Manuel. 2014. 'The High and the Low in the Making of Portuguese National Cuisine in the Nineteenth and Twentieth Centuries'. In *Food Consumption in Global Perspective: Essays in the Anthology of Food in Honour of Jack Goody*, edited by Jakob Klein and Anne Murcott, 108–34. New York: Palgrave Macmillan.

Subrahmanyam, Sanjay. 1993. *The Portuguese Empire in Asia 1500–1700*. New York: Longman.

Sutton, David. 2001. *Remembrance of Repasts: An Anthropology of Food and Memory*. Oxford: Berg.

Tan, Chee-Beng. 2007. 'Nyonya cuisine: Chinese, non-Chinese and the Making of a Famous Cuisine in Southeast Asia'. In *Food and Foodways in Asia: Resource, Tradition and Cooking*, edited by Sidney Cheung and Chee-Beng Tan, 171–82. Abingdon: Routledge.

Taylor Sen, C. 1996. 'The Portuguese Influence on Bengali Cuisine'. In *Food on the Move: Proceedings of the Oxford Symposium on Food and Cookery*, edited by H. Walker, 288–98. London: Prospect Books.

Watson, James. 1977. *Between Two Cultures: Migrants and Minorities in Britain*. Oxford: Basil Blackwell.

Webster, Pereira, D. 2012. 'How Can You Be Portuguese?' *UMA News Bulletin* (January–March): 1–5.

West, Michael Lee. 1999. *Consuming Passions: A Food-Obsessed Life*. New York: HarperCollins.

Wilk, Richard. 2002. 'Food and Nationalism: The Origins of "Belizean Food"'. In *Food Nations: Selling Taste in Consumer Societies*, edited by Warren Belasco and Philip Scranton, 67–89. New York: Routledge.

Wilk, Richard. 2006. *Home Cooking in the Global Village: Caribbean Food from Buccaneers to Ecotourists*. New York: Berg.

Wilk, Richard, and Livia Barbosa. 2012. *Rice and Beans: A Unique Dish in a Hundred Places*. London: Berg.

Wong, Julie. 2003. *Nyonya Flavours: A Complete Guide to Penang Straits Chinese Cuisine*. Penang: The State Chinese (Penang) Association; Salangor: Star Publications (M) Berhad.

Yoshino, Kosaku. 2010. 'Malaysian Cuisine: A Case of Neglected Culinary Globalization'. In *Globalization, Food and Social Identities in Asia Pacific Region*, edited by James Farrer, 1–15. Tokyo: Sophia University Institute of Comparative Culture.

Zhang, Yang, and Michael Hitchcock. 2014. 'The Chinese Female Tourist Gaze: A Netnography of Young Women's Blogs on Macao'. *Current Issues in Tourism*. DOI: 10.1080/13683500.2014.904845.

Zhang, Yang, and C. L. Pang. 2012. 'From Home Food to Macanese Cuisine, Historical Development, Tourist Branding and Cultural Identity'. *Sociology Study* 2, no. 12: 934–40.

www.ingramcontent.com/pod-product-compliance
Ingram Content Group UK Ltd.
Pitfield, Milton Keynes, MK11 3LW, UK
UKHW021828140426
5217IPUK00017B/1259